Social Media Simplified

Highlights of the Book

- Analysis of the user preferences that have evolved over a period of time with technology causing the paradigm shifts in consumer behavior.
- Perspective on the concept of social media, it's utility for purposes beyond business and the key aspects of social media strategy.
- Specific insights (Do's, Don'ts) about 'Social Media Behavior' on Twitter & Facebook for both personal and business usage.
- Outline of the entrepreneurial and job opportunities that have emerged in this field.
- Discussion on the ways to measure the social media impact.
- Interpretation of the social media strategy being adopted by 30 brands operating in India across various sectors.

Social Media Simplified

Twitter, Facebook—Beyond Casual Networking

Vijayendra Haryal
Anandan Pillai

Ocean Paperbacks

A Division of Ocean Books Pvt. Ltd.

ISO 9001:2008 Publishers

Published by
Ocean Paperbacks
A Division of Ocean Books Pvt. Ltd.
4/19 Asaf Ali Road,
New Delhi-110 002 (INDIA)

ISBN 978-81-8430-105-2
Social Media Simplified
by **Vijayendra Haryal & Anandan Pillai**

Edition
First, 2011

Price
Rs. 150.00 (Rs. One Hundred Fifty Only)

Printed at
Bhanu Printers, Delhi

"What you have learnt is just a handful of sand,
What you have not, is as big as this world"

(English adaptation of a Tamil proverb by the renowned poet Avvaiyar[1])

Vijayendra is grateful to God for the journey of this book and the tremendous amount of learning in the process.

Anandan would like to dedicate this book to his grandfather who was a renowned Tamil Poet.

PROLOGUE

The authors of this book met each other in June 2007 at the Indian Institute of Management, Ahmedabad (IIMA). At that time Vijayendra was a second year student and Anandan was working as an Academic Associate at the institute. They were in touch for about three months and with the end of that course, Anandan moved on to assist another faculty and they hardly met each other thereafter. Vijayendra graduated from the institute in March 2008 and both of them lost touch with each other for almost two years. Then in 2010, one fine day Anandan saw Vijayendra's photo in the suggested friends section of Facebook. He was skeptical about sending a friend request, as they didn't share even a friendship at IIMA (in fact were just acquaintances for only three months). However, he went ahead and sent a friend request .To his surprise Vijayendra accepted it. So, they were reconnected with each other after two years via Facebook. At that time, Vijay was working in Chennai and Anandan was pursuing his PhD at Gurgaon. Though they were located at two ends of the country, social media helped them communicate. Gradually they got along well and while conversing began to notice that both of them had a keen interest in social media.

Anandan was pursuing his PhD and focused on social media as a domain for his thesis. He shared articles, presentations, videos and various other content related to social media on his Facebook profile. Vijayendra used to '*like*' (in the Facebook way) them, and they often had conversations relating to what Anandan posted. Sometimes they agreed with each other, and sometimes they had a difference of opinion. However the spirit of discussing with each other never ended. In the meantime, they realized that it would be a good idea to put together a detailed content resource on social media suited for an Indian audience and thus the idea of this book was born.

One may wonder how both the authors communicated with each other as physically they were located at two ends of the country. Believe it or not, they both communicated by cellphone only ONCE after deciding to agree on putting the book together. All later communications were made using Facebook and e-mail (sometimes chat) till almost 80 percent of the book was completed. They shared documents on Google Docs and made extensive use of social media to discuss and share content. It was not that they deliberately planned to work in this manner, but their work schedules didn't permit them to have voice conversations. When one of them used to stumble upon a good idea, he used to mail the other about it instead of losing the thought. Asynchronous communications played a key role in putting the book together. During those Internet communications, they not only exchanged professional notes, but also often used to communicate with each other about events in their professional and personal lives like going for a vacation, busy with assignments, the weather in their respective cities, festivities, food etc.

The knowledge spectrum of Indian audiences spans a wide range—on one extreme are the relatively few tech geeks, who are abreast of global technology trends, and on the other extreme, are the majority, who know little about technology. However everyone is increasingly becoming aware that technology can help them increase their productivity. Social media, amongst all technological trends, is the one which is touching just about everyone and thus it becomes important for all to understand this reasonably well. The purpose of the book is to demystify this domain in simple terms for the mass audience in India at the least possible cost, so that they don't remain disadvantaged as compared to others across the world. This book also contains keen insights on the subject which would help almost anyone to become more aware of, and use social media more effectively to his or her benefit.

So, don't hesitate to go social if you haven't yet! Enter the social world and enjoy the journey! All insights/suggestions/observations are based on the author's experiences and may/may not sound right to you. So if you disagree with anything, please feel free to write to them. Both of them are very eager to get the discussion rolling. Who knows these discussions might result in an improvised next edition of this book!

Happy Reading!

—Vijayendra & Anandan

PS: You must wonder why this section is written in the third person in the form of a story. It is not to pat ourselves on the back, but to exhibit a real life experience of how virtual life is fast empowering the real life. In today's world the physical constraints of sharing knowledge or working on a project together have been overcome largely by social media. It's a distant possibility that without the social media we would have ever connected with each other, leave aside putting this book together, as we hadn't even exchanged our email address or phone numbers/co-ordinates at IIMA. More importantly, we want to drive home the point that the names in the story above can be that of you and your colleague or friend working on an idea that ignites your passion!

PREFACE

The knowledge spectrum of Indian audiences spans a wide range—on one extreme are relatively few tech geeks, who are at par with the global technology trends, and on the other extreme, are the majority, who know little about technology. However, everyone is slowly but certainly becoming aware of the ways in which technology can help them increase their productivity. Social media, amongst all technological trends, is the one which is touching just about everyone and thus it becomes important to understand this reasonably well for all. In today's world irrespective of physical location, by using social media one can get tremendous information and communicate with almost anybody around the world. This book attempts to demystify this domain in simpler terms for the mass audience in India at the least possible cost, so that they don't remain disadvantaged and are more aware about its effective usage. This book also contains keen insights on the subject and has case studies which will be helpful for the industry practitioners and students keen to understand social media or pursue it as a career.

Social media has created a buzz across the world and recently created its impact in India too. With an increasing number of tech savvy youngsters in this country, it is expected that the social media adoption would increase in leaps and bounds. Interestingly, firms too are aggressively forming social media strategies to tap this new powerful democratized medium. This book is an attempt to educate the social media users (individuals and brands) about the key aspects and subtle nuances of this medium. Also, this book could act as an eye opener for the social media users who knowingly or unknowingly may not be using the medium appropriately. This book includes 30 case studies on brands operating in India encompassing 10 categories, which could provide the readers wealth of information on how brands are presently leveraging the medium to the utmost benefit. A brief on each chapter is detailed below:

Chapter 1: **Introduction:** A crisp brief of changing behavioral pattern of the Indian audience in terms of diminishing attention spans, technology enabled fast pace life, customized content preference, increased urge to gain identity and the like has been discussed. This purpose of this chapter is to stimulate the thought process on how rapidly the world has changed and India is not left behind certainly. This may trigger an introspection whereby you realize how the behavioral patterns have been evolving with the technological advancements and their impact on you.

Chapter 2: **What is Social Media?:** The concept of Social Media is explored in this chapter. Also, the key tenets of the phenomenon, classification of social media websites, and key websites like Facebook, Twitter, LinkedIn, etc. are discussed. This chapter will help the reader understand the social media domain and the various key aspects related to it.

Chapter 3: **Demystifying Twitter &** *Chapter 4:* **Demystifying Facebook:** These chapters highlight the key features of the two most prominent social media websites Twitter and Facebook; which is followed by a list of specific Dos and Don'ts for both individual users and the brands who are either using these websites or plan to use them in future. These chapters would help individual users to understand how to use Twitter & Facebook in a better and professional manner. The purpose is also to sensitize those who use it in a very casual manner about the risks of hurting their social image.

Chapter 5: **How Lives are Changing on a Personal Basis:** This chapter unravels the different facets of life which have undergone a significant change like relationships, recognition, diminishing attention spans, decreasing proximity with increasing online interaction, so on and so forth.

***Chapter 6:* How Should Firms Frame Their Social Media Strategy?**

An appropriate strategic approach should be followed by brands when they decide to enter the social media arena. This chapter enlists the various key questions that brands should ponder on while planning their social media entry. A detailed discussion on various aspects is provided, which would help brands decide their social media strategy in a comprehensive manner.

***Chapter 7:* Social Media ROI – Measuring Success:** The ROI from social media could be formulated in various forms, i.e. ROI related to business, ROI related to social media efforts per se, ROI related to community engagement etc.. Hence, considering ROI in social media as a single perspective would be an incomplete understanding, which is highlighted in this chapter. Metrics are proposed to measure the effectiveness of 'influence' which is directly linked to ROI.

***Chapter 8:* Social Media Utility Beyond Business:** Social media's professional utility is often considered only for business. This chapter however details the various facets in which social media's adequate usage could reap phenomenal benefits. Some activities where social media could be used are personal branding, fund raising, event marketing, crowd sourcing, solving criminal cases etc.

***Chapter 9:* Social Media Influence & Opportunities:** Influence on 'ways of working' of different fields like journalism, marketing, recruitment, politics etc is analyzed This chapter also lists some of the key opportunities both from an entrepreneurial as well as a professional perspective that social media has thrown open..

***Chapter 10:* Case Studies:** This section of the book provides readers an idea of the social media strategy and tactics that have been adopted by brands operating in India on various social media websites. The selection of Indian brands was done deliberately so that readers of could easily visualize the brand and comprehend the basic aspects of the product category these brands represent. Thirty case studies are included from ten categories–book retailing, apparels, accessories, airlines, automobiles, FMCG, insurance, multiplexes, telecom service providers, and NGO.

Glossary: Every medium has its own culture and ways of communication. The Internet too has created a kind of communication culture which is adapted by most of the Internet users and used on daily. Also some of the commonly used 'jargon' is explained. Comprehensive lists, non-exhaustive though, have been created for 'lingo' and 'terminologies'.

Considering the fact that this is the first of its kind social media book in the Indian context, a few things could have been missed, which we encourage our readers to share with us. In order to facilitate the learning process between our readers and ourselves we have created a presence of this book on Facebook and Twitter, wherein we expect our readers to share their learnings and criticisms which would be wholeheartedly entertained and responded to by both authors. Our Facebook page is 'Social Media Simplified' and Twitter handle is '@smsbeyond'.

CONTENTS

1

INTRODUCTION

You may have noticed that when you switch on the TV nowadays, you find a marked increase in channels and also a marked differentiation in content as compared to what existed a decade ago. From just the national channels about 25 years ago, to hundreds of private channels now, the viewers are spoilt for choice. The very fact that seldom a channel shuts down because of low profitability provides credence to the fact that most of them have a viable business model. The extent of viewership a channel is able to attract may differ, but there exists a niche market for different categories of content offered by each. Further, in a particular category sub-categories are constantly evolving. For example, for news channels, there are business news channels; in sports there are channels dedicated to cricket and so on. Not just in the electronic media, in almost all other fields like transport, communication, banking etc. user choices have evolved. The 'one size fits all' is an almost extinct phenomena. Users have a distinct need and preference for content and medium through which it is delivered (e.g. on internet, TV, mobile) to them. New business models to serve these opportunities are rapidly evolving. The old is getting replaced by the new at a phenomenal pace.

The behavioral change in the audience has resulted in a change in their preferences. They have become more 'participative' than 'passive' viewers. The inclination especially of the younger generation can be seen more towards 'reality' rather than 'fiction' (soap operas etc). In a typical 'entertainment' channel, the number of reality shows has increased. The highest Television Rating Points (TRPs) are commanded by some of the most popular reality shows like 'KBC (*Kaun Banega Crorepati*)', 'Indian Idol, ' Big Boss' and other reality shows. A distinct shift in consumer behavior is observed in movies too. Movies like *Peepli Live*, *No One Killed Jessica*, *Dhobi Ghat* etc though did not necessarily have a mass appeal but still attracted niche audiences and were profitable. There seems to be a growing demand for movies which are closer to real life.

This paradigm shift in preferences to a large extent can be attributed to technology. No longer does one need to stand in long queues to pay their utility bills, get a demand draft made at a bank or book movie, train or air tickets. Each of these and many more such activities can be done via the Internet sitting at the convenience of home or on the move through mobile, at any place and time comfortable to the user. Technology has made life much easier and faster. This has resulted in the reduced levels of patience levels in people and the simultaneous scaling up of diversified demands like never before. People today have begun to get frustrated even with the time it takes for the computer to boot, leave aside to download a movie or song.

Everything is now just a click or a call away. More so, now the customer's convenience is the top priority (for which the customer is ready to shell out extra charges), catered very efficiently and in a reliable manner with the help of technology. You can now even determine where you want to sit in a movie theatre, bus or an airplane while booking your tickets. There are so many products and service providers available now and everyone craves your attention. Internet has removed information asymmetry to a great extent. Now you can compare prices of almost anything you want to buy, from household goods to a broadband connection to holidays!

It's now imperative for all the firms, whether they operate in a B2C (Business to Consumer) or B2B (Business to Business) environment, to have some sort of social media presence, which could be on any of these – Twitter, Foursquare, Facebook, Linkedin, blog etc.. From a firm's perspective, their existing and prospective customers are, in most cases present on these websites and they are discussing about various brands. Firms need to play the crucial role of listening to these conversations and make use of them . Avoiding these is not

an option as competitors might take the proactive step to observe the conversations and get benefitted. Now discount offers are 'tweeted' and so are consumer grievances. Reviews are read with equal interest for movies as well as products and services. A bad review may cause a dent and create havoc for any business. The sensitivity to serve a customer well has magnified tremendously. This has lead to an increased sense of importance amongst individuals. Everyone wants to be heard, appreciated and wants to make his/her presence felt

With the arrival of social media (*explained in detail in Chapter 2*), now you can also converse (demand information, ask for clarifications etc) and negotiate with the brand, without even stepping into showrooms. Also, you can collect abundant information from customers who have had past experiences with the product. It is not necessary for you to know the person from whom you would be receiving help. The democratization of information acts as a bridge connecting people who you don't know. There are people on the Internet that may possess the information that you are looking for. All you need to do is raise the question and on getting answers use prudence in finding the information that is credible. An interesting point to note is that though there is a knowledge transaction which happens in this new media at every second, there is hardly any financial transaction between the information disseminators and information receivers.

When technology can cause such a radical shift and is constantly changing lives for better, people building or propagating the same are likely to benefit the most. Many a tale of young entrepreneurs now comes to light and most of these achievers who have taken a considerably short time to make it big in life have a technology related business. Mark Zuckerberg, CEO and co-founder of Facebook is an outstanding example. As of July, 2010, 500 million[1] (50 *crore*) people across the world were actively using Facebook. Taking into account the fact that Facebook was founded in February 2004, this is an astonishing feat! More and more people are joining Facebook at a rapid pace and, 26 year old Zuckerberg was named TIME[2] Person of the year 2010. The magnitude of this achievement can be understood by getting to know some of the others named TIME person of the year in this decade—Barack Obama (2008), Vladimir Putin (2007) and George W. Bush (2004)[3]. Even in the Indian context, 'working smart' is the new mantra as compared to putting in long hours. Now a considerable number of the young graduates working in an Indian IT company can book a flat at a very young age (may be early thirties or in some cases late twenties too!). This is speeded up even more if this young professional gets to work onsite. The speed at which the world has moved can be understood from the fact that this was a life time achievement for most of their parents!

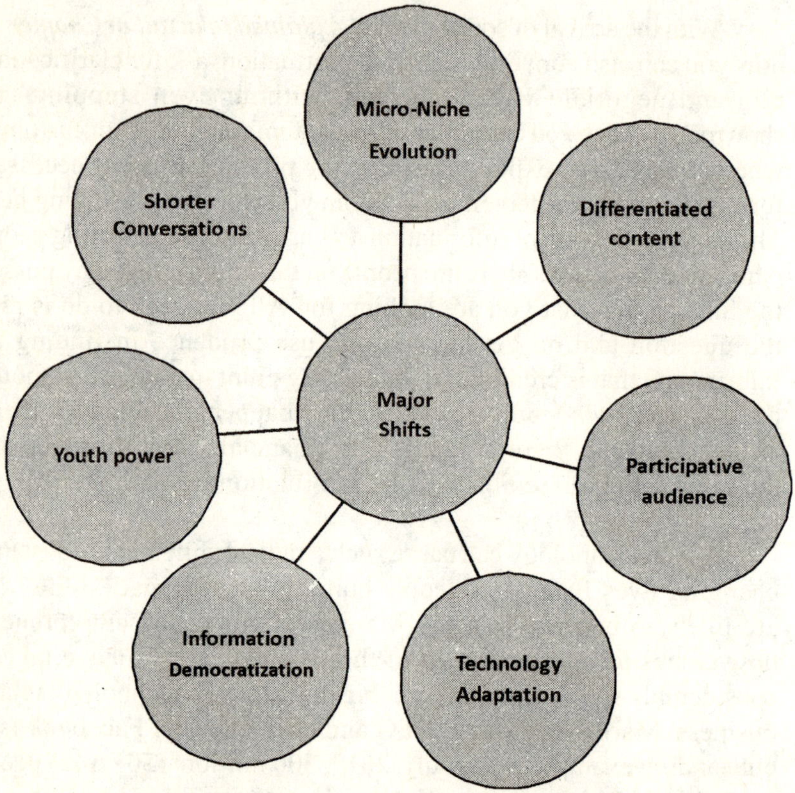

Fig. 1: Major Shifts in Consumer Behavior

Another interesting phenomenon is the change in the way in which communications are taking place both online and otherwise. Everything is now communicated in as few words as possible with the use of as many abbreviations, especially in the online world. The abbreviations also wary a wide range; like 2U2 is short for 'to you too' whereas WYSIWYG elaborates to 'What You See Is What You Get'. The deeper implication is that not only people's patience to listening has gone down, but the same has happened to the patience with respect to speaking. They want to be understood in as a brief a communication (and hence time) as possible. This trend has been catered to effectively by the website Twitter which facilitates micro blogging. If you have yet not started using it, once you register or Sign Up, you can create your profile and post updates (short messages) which are known as tweets. These tweets are text based messages which can be a maximum of 140 characters. If you subscribe to someone else's tweets, you are known as a *follower* and this is known as *following*. As of September 14, 2010[4] Twitter had some 175 million (17 *crore* 50 *lakh*) registered users and 95 million (9 *crore* 50 *lakh*) tweets per day.

Advancements in technology in a subtle but very profound way have caused behavioral shifts. The key to 'unlocking' the 'technology potential' and use it for maximum business benefit is to understand these 'behavioral shifts' and tailor the products, services and marketing strategy to address these. This book is an attempt towards understanding the Indian user, demystifying the tools and technologies which may be utilized effectively to further and achieve business and personal goals. The case studies from various sectors included in the book give a perspective to the social media presence of the corporate houses and the ways in which brands make an effort to approach you every time you are logged in.

Though the authors have shared their insights and observations throughout the book, the reader is encouraged to analyze and think from an independent viewpoint.

□

2

WHAT IS SOCIAL MEDIA?

The purpose of the media, simply put is to disseminate information, and in the process entertain, communicate and most importantly form opinions and change society's attitude. Information can be conveyed in any form, like voice, document, picture, video, etc. Today's generation can look back and definitely realize the path that media has travelled and the transformations it has passed through. Even before human beings could invent the basic post or telegraph services, information was disseminated and received with the help of animals (e.g. pigeons) and fellow human beings who carried information and conveyed it to the receiver. The gradual technological innovations gave rise to a flood of innovations like post, print, telegraph, radio, television, mobile and Internet. After Internet, have you pondered what is the next big innovation related to media that transformed the way human beings conversed with each other?

Even before you try to answer this question, you should contemplate that most of the media technologies were invented with a social purpose. Business entities always found a way to utilize the medium to reach customers and spread their message. Now, did human beings object to such intrusion? Yes, no, maybe—the answer would vary from person to person based on their experiences. A person who has been often harassed by unwanted phone calls from insurance and credit card companies would definitely support the thought of minimizing and if possible eliminating these intrusions. Someone who has been benefitted by receiving the relevant information which may have helped him or her in personal life may highly endorse this dissemination of knowledge.

Before analyzing the commercial value of the social media, let's understand why the social media wave has swept all human beings across the world much faster than any of the earlier media exchange phenomena. What's so unique about it that has enabled its penetration at such a tremendous speed?

Why is it called social media?

Let's first look at how the Internet has evolved. In the initial phases, web pages were used to just convey information thus involving a passive interaction. Content was simple and conveyed in a more or less monotonous way. Gradually, 'User Interface' started gaining more importance. Web pages still having a passive interface now were made attractive with designs that users found exciting and made them stay on the web page longer. Fast forward to this date and you will realize that the Internet is no longer passive. Users now interact with each other, post comments on every article they read, write reviews of the places they visit and dine, share their photos with friends etc. In short, users have started interacting, unlike just sitting and watching TV or reading a newspaper passively. As the content is generated and evolves within the social network spontaneously the connotation 'social media' is appropriate. Secondly, as all such users are now connected with each other, and hence can now converse with each other much faster and easily this makes the present media social to a great extent.

The new wave of media has probably increased the user's span of control versus the earlier versions of media and it has also reduced the intrusion level thus connecting billions of people all around the world. Previously, a particular person could reach only those whom he/she knew well, or had met at least once in a lifetime. These relationships are often referred to as strong ties[1]. So, whatever conversations happened, they had a boundary to it and there existed a one to one correspondence. Many to one correspondence did gather momentum via mails and phone calls but were limited to the 'circle of trust' or the ones that you were acquainted with. This was the case with post, telephone, mobile etc. However, Internet redefined these boundaries, which benefited the business arena as well as personal lives to a great extent. Earlier avatars of the Internet still posed some amount of restriction on the extent to which users could meet people across the length and breadth of the earth. Moreover, earlier, people did not have platforms like those which exist today where they can converse in open and discuss their feelings amongst fellow users. Technically, users had some facilitation to spread word of mouth using Internet but their capability to influence someone's choice was limited.

Then came the technological innovations that facilitated the asynchronous communications, and all of a sudden people realized that now they were equipped to share their views and also share it with anyone across the world. So, the fundamental requirement of 'knowing' a person was done away. With the technology enablement to share, reach a wider audience and complete the day-to-day tasks much faster, people are becoming more actively 'connected' through the social media.

Sharing – The fulcrum of social media phenomena

In the social media world, one has the possibility to reach out and communicate with any person in the world. Building an identity in the society has been a priority for people and this need has increased further over a period of time. In earlier days, one could become a well-known personality only if the person was a famous politician, sport star, industrialist, film star etc. All other people with comparatively lesser popularity had huge hurdles to cross for building their image. However, with the arrival of social media, these untraced traits got varied channels to exhibit their talent and gain popularity. Hence, the focus has considerably shifted from "who you are?" to "what you do?"/"what you know?" More than the talent one possesses, what has fuelled the process of recognition is the 'sharing' phenomenon. Social media channels enable people to spread the word about the content they see, immediately and to a wide number of people. There is a win-win situation. One who shares the content is also gaining 'something' by making it available to his friends. When someone shares content, the receiver may do one or more of the following:

1. Appreciate the intentions of the person who has shared the content.

2. Perceive that the person who shared the content is well aware of the subject.
3. As it was shared by someone (and especially if it is from someone who you know), the probability to trust it would be very high.

Hence, the entire phenomenon of "I share with you, you share it with him, he/she will share with others." spreads like wildfire thanks to technology. It is a win-win situation for everyone in the loop, however at the end of the day, the person at the fulcrum benefits by reaching the widest audience at the minimal effort and cost. Let's see what all could be shared on social media, and where lies the business prospect.

What & where can be shared?

In the traditional media, there were specific modes for sharing specific type of content—for instance TV for audio/visual content, newspaper for text, radio for audio, billboards for text on the move etc. However, Internet and the social media channels that followed have enabled people to share a variety of content online. The content could be a word file, a photo, a music file, a video file, a podcast, live voice, etc. As the phenomenon developed, many websites have emerged and positioned themselves as unique channel to share a particular type of content. The social media could be classified based on the social objective around which the value proposition is offered (Table 1).

An individual user should match his/her objectives and the value offered by the website, before planning their presence on it. Although, there have been cases when a contact made or reestablished through 'Relationship SNWs' has resulted in business or professional gains, these instances are few and far between. These 'lateral gains' can be explored depending on the bandwidth (with respect to time) you have. It has been observed that people usually avoid keeping their colleagues and especially bosses from their workplace added into their social networks. This can be observed as a healthy practice as you get your personal space and express feelings in an environment of trusted people and those who you are well acquainted with. Besides getting to know

Table 1: Classification of social media

Key value proposition	*Examples*
Social networking	Facebook, MySpace, Orkut, Bigadda, Indyarocks, Ibibo, hi5, etc.
Professional networking	LinkedIn, XING, Ryze etc.
Photo sharing	Flickr, etc.
Video sharing	YouTube, Vimeo, etc.
Document sharing	Slideshare, Docstoc, Scribd
Social Bookmarks	Delicious, StumbleUpon
Blog platforms	Blogspot, Wordpress
Location based networks	TripIt, Foursquare
SMS	SMSGupshup, Way2sms etc.
Microblogs	Twitter
Virtual World	SecondLife, GoJiyo
Crowdsourced content	Redditt, Digg

the personal details (achievements, relocation, marriage, anniversary etc) of your group of friends instantly, some of them who you may not be in regular contact with, social media is also about sharing knowledge and in the process harnessing the potential of the society as a whole. The basic rule of knowledge holds true here too—"The more you share, the more you gain". However what, when, how to share for optimizing your exposure and maximizing gain needs to be dealt with utmost care. The same has been dealt with later in the book extensively.

A detailed discussion on all social media channels available in this world would be beyond the scope of this book. Brief details about some of the major social media channels, which are being used extensively by a large number of users is given below. These social media channels have a unique purpose, which should be understood both by individual users and the brands.

Facebook: Facebook was founded in 2004 by Mark Zuckerberg[2]. Facebook had over 500 million unique users across the world as of July, 2010[3]. Facebook can be used to build, maintain relationships with known or unknown acquaintances. First time Facebook users can find their friends on the channel with the help of their email address, whereby Facebook searches for people whose email address is there on your email. The users can post about their daily activities, share their emotions in the space provided, which is referred to as *wall.* Users can also share their photos, videos with their friends. Facebook has numerous (thousands or even more) of applications related to various themes like business, education, entertainment, games, lifestyle, fun, sports utilities etc[4]. A firm/brand can create its presence on Facebook, with the Facebook Pages[5] feature, and also create a community of their customers, employees etc. to interact with them. It can then update the community members by posts on its Facebook page. As soon as it makes a post on the Facebook page, it would appear on the wall of every community member of this Facebook page. Any user could make use of Facebook Groups[6] feature to form a close group of friends to have personal interaction.

Twitter: Twitter is a real time information sharing network founded in 2006[7]. It had around 175 million unique users as of September 2010[8]. Individual users can build their Twitter profile by providing key information in the *Bio* section. Also, users can make use of their blog or networking website *weblink* in the Web section, to share detailed information about them. In Twitter users can share their tweets (short messages of 140 characters) with their followers. Twitter is considered to be pretty *viral* in nature and information travels very fast through this channel. A firm/brand can also create its Twitter account and engage with the customers. A key feature of Twitter is *trendlist*, which displays the topics on which large number of Twitter users are tweeting at a particular given time period. Twitter users while tweeting can make use of hashtag (#) with certain keywords in their tweets, so that these tweets get aggregated with those by other people who tweeted on same keyword. Users can also search for certain keywords using hashtag and join discussions that happen around the topic to which the hashtag is related.

LinkedIn: LinkedIn founded in 2003, is a professional networking channel with over 90 million registered users across 200 countries[9]. LinkedIn offers a common platform for firms and professionals to meet and connect with each other. Users can build their professional profile on this website, containing details about their education, professional experience details etc. This website is increasingly being used by recruiters to find appropriate candidates and sometimes also for reference checks. Like other social media channels, users can also change their status message on LinkedIn. LinkedIn includes features like LinkedIn Answers[10], where users can ask questions regarding their professional life and have them answered by experts who are present on the channel. LinkedIn Groups[11] is a very helpful feature, by which groups on various themes exist on the LinkedIn. Users can join groups of their interest interact with the professionals present on that group and upgrade themselves in various ways. LinkedIn Jobs[12] feature can be used by individual job seekers to find relevant jobs for them. Also firms can post jobs using this feature. Firms can also create their Company Pages[13] on LinkedIn sharing details like key statistics, firm description, products, employees, etc. to build the image of the firm amongst the professional users. Any customer, prospective employee can go through this page and have updated information about the firm and share it further with his/her network.

YouTube: YouTube founded in 2005 is a video sharing channel which had over 2 billion views a day as of May, 2010[14]. Users can watch videos on varied topics, *like* them, comment on those videos, share them with their network etc. Firms can create their presence on YouTube with the help of Channels feature. Firms can create their detailed profile and share videos of their firm on this channel. Any individual can subscribe to brand's YouTube channel and receive updates about videos uploaded by the brand.

Slideshare: Slideshare is a document sharing channel where a user can share presentations, documents, pdfs. Slideshare is growing with 25 million visitors and attracted 70 million pageviews monthly[15]. Documents uploaded on Slideshare have the potential to spread virally on Facebook, Twitter and LinkedIn. Firms/brands can create their presence on Slideshare and share presentations, documents, which can be informative for their employees or external stakeholders. Users can embed Slideshare with their blog or website. Like other social media channels, Slideshare too has groups formed on varied themes.

It ought to be noted that social media channels have certain features in common like user profile, comments section, sharing feature, uploading various forms of content, groups etc. These features enable individual users and firms/brands to share content, discuss with their stakeholders, which results in substantial information sharing amongst the users. There are many such channels and readers of this book are recommended to explore and find the right kind of channel that would suit their needs. □

3

DEMYSTIFYING TWITTER

Simply put, the basic concept behind Twitter can be identified as a modern version of short messaging service (SMS) channel with some added features. Your *followers* on Twitter are the people, who choose to be updated with the *tweets (*the post or message displayed on your profile page) you share, when you *follow someone,* you decide to be updated with tweets of that person. Besides sharing information like text, videos, pictures etc, this channel can also be used for exploring relationships (business or personal) with people who you may not know otherwise. It is the easiest and the fastest way to update all in one's network about what one wants to convey and also to receive updates from others about what's happening in their lives, have access to what the others share.

If you are looking forward to sustain your followers in the long term, it's very important that you tweet the content relevant and of interest to them. The tweets made by a person would reach the timeline of his/her followers instantaneously. Instead if one needs to communicate with a specific person, he/she could use the *Direct Message (DM)* feature, wherein one could tweet to that particular person, and none of the other followers would be updated about this tweet. Also, if one doesn't want to explicitly *follow* a person, but has an inherent motivation to receive updates from that person, he/she could make use of *Lists* feature, wherein one could add people to the list (similar to that of labels feature in Gmail) and one can regularly visit these lists to check the updates.

The 'tweet' has to be worded in just 140 characters! Be it a company or a person, the message has to be well drafted, to convey accurately and grab attention, with the challenge of putting it together in just these few characters. This channel has also been used efficiently by individuals to promote themselves, their blogs, their professional and personal achievements etc. Like other social networking channels, Twitter empowers individuals to build their identity in the virtual world. Listed below are some tips (*Do's*) that can help individuals build their social identity using Twitter. Also listed is behavior which should be avoided (*Don'ts*) to have a valuable experience on this channel. Please note that this is not an exhaustive list of *Do's* and *Don'ts* but surely covers some of the most important ones.

If you are yet to use Twitter or even if you are already using it, it would be a good idea to browse through http://support.twitter.com/ to understand more about the features and their judicious use.

Twitter Do's and Don'ts for individuals

Do's

1) Prepare an authentic bio

Anyone on the internet, who is unknown to you and by some chance lands at your Twitter handle, is likely to first go through your bio. It is the only source of information to judge your credibility and which may decide if the person is going to *follow* you or not. Also, given the limitation on the character space to express yourself, you should make judicious use of words to present the information. The most likely information that could gain interest is your profession and key interests. It would be advisable not to include lingo/jargon (like "geek", "cool" etc) to describe oneself if you want to use Twitter for a serious purpose (business networking, building a brand etc). Also, it's absolutely essential that you state your real name and preferably upload a recent picture of yours.

2) Follow relevant people

Twitter has certain restrictions on number of people one could follow. Once a person follows 2,000 people, he/she may not be allowed to follow any further people unless the ratio of *following/followers* meets certain criteria set by Twitter[1]. When you chose to "*follow*" someone on Twitter, your *timeline* (Twitter updates from people you *follow*) includes the updates from this person. Instead of just about following as many famous personalities as possible, you should have a defined focus and follow relevant people. *Following* excessive number of people may clutter your timeline and create confusion. Even in an area of interest like social media, business or sports, it would be sometimes difficult to identify relevant people at the first go, but *following* them for certain period of time, you can decide which of them are sharing information that is relevant or interesting to you. So it's good to be selective and keep reviewing the list of people to ensure that you *follow* only those who are adding value as sought by you. It's strongly recommended that, you should *follow* major personalities in one's field, to remain updated about the field. This will help you in best utilization of your time on twitter.

3) Acknowledge every source

When you are *tweeting* (posting an update on Twitter) or *retweeting* (sharing an update posted by someone whom you are following, further to your followers), you should acknowledge the source from where the information is retrieved. The source could be a blog, news portal, or even an offline magazine or newspaper. This reaffirms your belief in ethics and will create a positive impression on those in your network. It becomes more vital in case you are *retweeting* a particular *tweet*. This builds your credibility in the minds of the source and there are chances that person will start *following* you. Also, if you appreciate a particular *tweet*, you should make it a point to thank that person and acknowledge his/her efforts.

4) Use appropriate hashtags

Hashtags (#<word>) are an important feature of Twitter which facilitates searching the information you seek in the vast ocean of numerous *tweets*. Someone who is searching for information related to a particular topic will search for appropriate *hashtags*. Hence, when you are tweeting about an event, person, etc. use of *hashtags* should be encouraged. This increases the chances of your visibility in a particular area of discussion and would help you in gaining more followers.

5) Maintain focus on your domain

If someone is following you, the person most probably has certain expectation from you on a particular professional domain for e.g. mobile phone software, digital marketing, automobiles, financials etc. This expectation gets build based on the twitter bio you have prepared and the past history of *tweets*. Hence, it would be unjustified if one *tweets* on unrelated topics that may irritate the followers. One should ensure that quality information and steady *tweets* is provided with respect to one's field to fulfill the expectations of the followers. Else, one could easily notice that followers will start *unfollowing* (voluntarily stop receiving updates from you).

6) Engage with community

Tweeting doesn't mean one should involve in just one way bombarding of information on your followers. This would be just one way information flow and does not help a person to build relationship with others. Hence, when someone replies to your *tweet* or *retweets* or shows interest in the *tweet*, one should take this opportunity to engage with that person and build relationship with that person. In short two way information flow should be the objective. Showing gratitude when others appreciate what you post is a good starting point.

7) Use "direct message" feature judiciously

As of now the *"direct message"* (DM) feature is available only to those who you follow. By using this any of those that you follow can send a *DM* to you instead of posting on your timeline. This is an amazing feature, which guarantees privacy even on the social channel. It may not be advisable to get into argument with someone in open channel, or approach someone for some specific objective publically. In this case you should make it a point to use the *DM* feature and get into personal communication with the concerned person.

Don'ts

1) Don't automate

There are quite a few Twitter tools on the Internet, which could be used to automate one's account for variety of purposes. For instance automated applications are available to send a 'thank you' message to new *follower*, or to *unfollow* someone who has not been active for a certain period of time, or to stream *tweets* at regular intervals of time (this is often practiced when one has followers from different parts of the world) etc. Though it makes managing your Twitter account easy, it does not form a favorable impression. The personalization touch is lost with the usage of automated *tweets* using applications and the person on other side will be more often than not smart enough to differentiate an automated tweet and a real-time tweet.

2) Don't 'tweet' unnecessarily

Tweeting regularly is a desirable activity, however *tweeting* unnecessarily is not perceived positively. It may not be necessary to *tweet* what you're eating, or who are you going for a date with and more such extremely personal information. This may result in privacy issues and also cause your *followers* to lose interest.

3) Don't 'retweet' unnecessarily

You might be very interested in someone's *tweet*. It doesn't mean you *retweet* everything that this 'someone' tweets to your own *followers*. Your interest might not necessarily match that of your followers, so you should avoid *retweeting* unnecessarily and avoid spamming timeline of your followers.

4) Don't tweet personal messages on your professional account

If you are an author, freelancer, consultant etc. most of your followers might be interested in your professional domain and not in your personal life aspects. So you should avoid tweeting about personal life on professional account. It would look unprofessional to tweet about personal life on professional account.

5) Don't get involved in unnecessary arguments

If by some reason you end up in an awkward situation of someone picking on you, don't get into arguments in public. In the heat of the moment you might write some untoward words, which might impact your image and send across wrong message to followers. Hence, it is advisable to pacify the situation and intimate openly that you would like to have a personal communication with the person who has created this situation. In order to avoid such arguments/awkward situations tweets regarding a person's religion, relationships, career, salaries, professional issues etc shall be avoided.

6) Don't urge people to follow you

In order to have good amount of followers, some people try hard to convince their friends and people around to *follow* them (which is often referred to as *cyber bullying*). This is an absolutely unwarranted social activity and one should avoid this.

7) Don't delete your tweet

It just takes seconds for your tweet to reach the *timeline* of your hundreds or may be thousands of *followers*. So, if you delete a tweet from your *timeline*, it doesn't mean it won't reach the wider audience. Hence, if by mistake one has *tweeted* wrong (not the correct wordings etc) information, don't feel shy to apologize in public. Accepting the mistake will result in respect for you. We all make mistakes. However always remember the golden rule 'Think long enough before tweeting'. The *tweet* is like an arrow which is almost impossible to retrieve once shot!

Twitter Do's and Don'ts for firms/brands

Firms (a for-profit organization, or any other type of organization, including non-profit, non-government etc.) can have a Twitter handle for them or specific brands to engage with their customers. There is no special requirement, it is as simple as one needs to have a personal Twitter handle. However, in maintaining the firm's or brand's account special care needs to be taken, because after all it's managed by specific (or multiple) human beings. Though the interaction on behalf of the firm/brand is carried out by the executives, customers perceive it as 'personified' communication with the brand. The consistency in the message on behalf of the brand should be maintained. Conventionally, when a user has an issue/complaint about a product/service they talk to customer care representatives on phones and email. This is just a problem resolving approach, however social media is much more than just to answer customer queries or resolve customer complaints. It should be efficiently used to interact with customers, identify brand evangelizers, promote word of mouth for brand and enhance the positioning. Listed below are some of the key Do's and Don'ts for firm's or brand's Twitter handle, which the social media managers need to take care of.

Dos

1) Optimize your message well

Firms and brands would ideally love their customers to read tons of pages about them. The 'Twitter generation' however is very different. The Twitter users more often than not look forward to crisp information that would help them familiarize with the product/ promotion or for that matter anything else seeking their attention. Also, Twitter has a common rule for everyone, be it an individual or a brand, of 140 characters per *tweet* to communicate. So, firms/brands need to strategize their message accordingly and try to maximize the value of their message in the given restricted space. There may be a few iterations as you figure out what's working out and what's not. It's a good idea to therefore take feedback from internal as well as external sources *following* the brand or firm and work out a process of frequent checks and balances to ensure effective messaging.

2) Decide your objective

Twitter is just a channel or a stage where a brand can do whatever it likes to do. A brand might use it for providing product information, promoting new products, sourcing new ideas, handling queries, responding to complaints etc. Hence, a firm/brand needs to decide well in advance the objective it wishes to attain through Twitter and accordingly messages should be strategized. The messaging should not be cluttered as it may confuse those who follow the brand. The firm has to handle complaints, provide product information, feature promoting offers and give other relevant information. The priority of which information is to be shared/catered has to be decided based on customer's preferences and a firm's strategy. This would avoid cross-pollination of messages and keep the messaging focused.

3) Tweet relevant information

The followers of a brand/firm could be any of the stakeholders. It could be a stock broker, a supplier, a customer, legal advisor, or in fact even competitor brand. The brand should stick to the tweets related to its brand/firm rather than providing updates about weather, riots happening in the city etc. Tweeting such unrelated messages just to garner attention would indicate that firm/brand doesn't have enough content to be delivered to their followers, and it will not create a positive impression. A 'congratulatory' message on a famous victory in cricket can be a one off affair as this may add some 'personification' to the brand.

4) Use social media dashboards When firms/brands have multiple accounts, it would be advisable to make use of social media dashboards to maintain these multiple accounts. Dashboards are applications that allow community managers to manage multiple accounts on a single medium, with a single login. Some of the common dashboards used often in the industry are TweetDeck, Hootsuite, Ping.fm, Digsby etc. This would allow one to track the happenings on multiple accounts and react on real-time basis.

5) Be responsive to both positive and negative comments

One cannot expect customers to always shower praise on the firm/brand. There might be some unsatisfied customers out there in the market, or some intentional competitor agents who might be trying to bad mouth the brand. As it is a social channel everyone has a right to speak and express, so there could not be a legal way to curb such comments. The community manager needs special skills to handle such comments. Avoiding such comments might provoke the *tweeters* to *tweet* further, hence, one should try to clarify the brands response to a negative comment and apologize/rectify if there has been a genuine complaint case.

6) Identify appropriate brand evangelizers

This should be one of the major objectives of firm/brand to identify appropriate brand evangelizers, engage them in discussions and encourage them to spread word of mouth about the brand. These brand evangelizers need to be handled very carefully else, they might also be powerful enough to spread negative word of mouth.

7) Gain customer insights

In the process of discussions with customers, brand should consistently look for opportunities to improvise their offerings based on the constant feedback via Twitter. When such an opportunity arises, firm should make use of it and engage further with the customer to get to the depth of the issue.

Don'ts

1) Don't become too eager for followers

It may be easy for well known brands to attract huge crowd instantaneously and have a large number of followers. It might not be possible for a local brand or a regional brand to replicate this. But, it doesn't mean the brand should make untoward efforts like spamming to gain followers. A brand should respect others' privacy and accordingly make a suitable pitch.

2) Don't hard sell

One should not ideally look to Twitter only as a selling medium. Customers tend to get saturated of many channels through which a brand reaches them. They perceive Twitter as a unique form of communication and not yet another mode to disturb their privacy. So, this medium should be ideally used to listen, track and monitor the conversations about the brand, which often goes unnoticed through other medium. You may '*tweet*' about some special discounts and new product launches but should not try to 'overdo' the selling else, users might perceive your Twitter handle as a yet another selling medium.

3) Don't tweet remarks on your competitor

Like in any other public forum, a brand should restrain from commenting on competitor's brands. This would create very wrong impression in the customer's mind. And, if the competitor brand retaliates, it would be damaging both the brands, with no one gaining anything out of this 'tit-for-tat' exercise.

4) Don't tweet about yourself,

The community managers, who are handling the brand's Twitter handle, should be very careful while tweeting. Customers are following the account to know about the brand and not about the community manager. Hence, community managers should not make personal updates on their professional account. This would damage the impression of the brand.

5) Don't automate your tweets

Some firms try to automate their *tweets* with the help of various Twitter tools available on the Internet. It is not advisable to *tweet* via such automated *tweets*, as firms should always try to build a one-on-one relationship with each customer. Each customer should be individually addressed and sending automated *tweets* may be perceived as disrespectful by the customers who are following the brand. One more drawback is if a user posts negative remarks and there is an automated response, the user may feel further disgruntled. Therefore it is a must to customize and personalize the message, however always remember "Never to get involved into an argument on a public forum like Twitter." Get in personal contact with the user by a *direct message* and resolve the issue.

6) Don't make personal contacts

Some community managers may also tend to make personal contacts with the customers and use them for personal gain. It should not be allowed at any cost and strictly prohibited by the firm. The Twitter handle should only have the focus to build relationship with customer and brand.

7) Don't reveal key firm secrets

The community managers should also not reveal firm secrets on the Twitter handle, as there is high chance the competitors are following the brand. It might result in reducing differentiation for the firm. Twitter provides you an option to give permission to follow your tweets to only the people you approve. The moment you start using this option, your tweets will not be available publically.

□

4

DEMYSTIFYING FACEBOOK

Your social graph is determined by the quality of conversations, people on the network and information exchanged you and your network members. Hence, it's important to adopt some best practices (*Dos*) and refrain from indulging in certain kind of untoward behavior (*Don'ts*) while interacting on a day-to-day basis. Though, you may think that your posting does not make any difference on a 'casual' site like Facebook or MySpace, it all adds to your social image.

This social image building process may seem like a waste of time in the short term, but in the long run, this has the potential to yield rich dividends. For example, someone with whom you are interacting on Facebook can give you a lead to a potential job opening (may be his status update, it may be you reaching out to him outside Facebook etc) or in other case, someone may bounce a creative business idea and then you can team up and find a future business partner. Even someone's posts and views on particular topics may be liked by you and he/she may end up as a date and subsequently marriage. The social media is an opportunity to expand your network multiple times than is possible usually. It thus increases your 'probability' of doing something constructive with your network like the instances stated above. The flip side is, if not used judiciously and wisely, it can have negative consequences and result in harming your reputation. While each person has to determine his/her own 'positioning' in social network, listed below are some of the recommendations for personal online presence.

If you are yet to use Facebook or even if you are already using it, it would be a good idea to browse through http://www.facebook.com/

help/to understand more about the features and their judicious use.

Below is a list which includes some tips (*Do's*) that can help individuals build their social identity using social networking websites like Facebook. Also listed is behavior which should be avoided (*Don'ts*) to have a valuable experience on this channel. Please note that this is not an exhaustive list of *Do's* and *Don'ts* but surely covers some of the most important ones.

Facebook Do's and Don'ts for individuals

Do's

1) Reciprocate

Be generous in replying to peoples' comments on your posts. If someone took note of what you had to say, it's pretty obvious that they expect you also to take care of what they had to say and reciprocate. If you don't do that, chances are high that people will stop replying or even reading what you post. The reciprocation on Internet needs to be explicitly demonstrated; else the other person wouldn't have any clue, if you had even read his/her post.

2) Pay attention to the network's updates

Rather than just posting and replying to the people's comments on your posts, do read what others have written also and drop in a comment or '*like*' (Facebook allows you to express your liking by a '*like*' tab on each post) others post. This helps to develop a rapport between you and the other person and you will find that getting extended beyond the online life as well.

3) Keep track of important events/days

All networking websites post reminders of 'Birthday', 'Marriage Anniversary' and the like of those in your network. Drop in a good wish everyday on such occasions on that person's wall or send him a private message. Even if it's a busy day and you fail to do so, make sure you do it the next day. These occasions, are very special to every person and whosoever drops in even a small comment, captures the mindspace of the 'birthday boy' or the 'anniversary couple'. You would be pleasantly surprised to see numerous good wishes on your 'special occasions' – accelerating your social graph.

4) Link friends

Do recommend friends to your friends and help them 'connect' to those in your network, if your friend wants. This will help in the 'favour being returned' when you ask for. This will further your reach and expand your network.

5) Show Gratitude & Share

If you are benefitted in terms of knowledge by a link or a story or an update that a person has posted, you should thank him/her. This encouragement can lead to more such behavior and thus more knowledge sharing can take place. You should also post relevant content that you come across and who knows that a discussion on that may reveal some new insights!

6) Know likes/dislikes

Do post a link or story from a topic which is of specific interest to a friend on his/her wall. This will let that person have a special feeling that you care for him/her and will also establish a 'positive image' for you in your network as well as the others can see what you are posting.

7) Keep profile updated

Do keep your profile 'updated' regularly with all the necessary information like 'what you are looking for', 'your employer', your interests etc. This helps the relevant people to network and connect with you. Keep checking your privacy setting's (the people who you want to share info with etc) very carefully as you can control access to each micro bit of the information you share.

Don'ts

1) Don't add complete strangers

Do not accept a 'friend request' from anyone blindly who you have not known before. This can be really detrimental as that person may be a spammer or an unwanted entity. If you are not sure and still want to connect, you can send that person a personal message and inquire more about him/her before adding to your network.

2) Don't post confidential information

Do not post information which is confidential (e.g. a bid that your company is pursuing etc). This can be very detrimental to your career. It's also not recommended that you post negative views about your company as this is not taken in a positive light and to vent out your grievances, most of the companies now have internal portals.

3) Don't eschew privacy

Do not post about issues on the wall, which may be too personal to you or the person on whose wall you post. Postings regarding a person's religion, relationships, career, salaries, professional issues etc shall not be posted in public. Everything that you post on your wall/someone else's wall, automatically gets posted on everyone's wall in your network, unless you have some privacy settings

4) Don't post on contentious issues

Avoid posting on contentious issues especially those relating to a bias against a religion, sex, a country or a community. These are never taken in the stride and are bound to have negative effect on your image as a person with strong biases.

5) Don't nag

Do not nag a girl or a guy who you are interested in, if she or he is not interested by sending out messages/posting on the wall etc. There are strict cyber laws emerging in the Indian context too and you may find yourself in trouble if you are involved in indecent behavior.

6) Don't post impromptu videos/pictures

Be very careful while posting photos or videos in your profile. These can be easily downloaded and used against you or misinforming a prospective employer or spouse/date. For example photos from a 'wild party' can be detrimental to your own image in front of your family. For that matter please be cautious as who is clicking you as people are very eager to post all kinds of pictures on Facebook!

7) Don't click on any suspicious (unknown) link

Do not click on every application that your friend has "*liked*".

Some of the applications contain spam and they retrieve information about you, which could be used against you in some manner. Even some applications may damage your PC or laptop, as they may contain virus.

Facebook Do's and Don'ts for firms/brands

A Facebook page is a brand's profile on Facebook, similar to that of an individual's presence. However, this Facebook page has certain unique features like unlimited number of community members, access to applications, access to analytics, etc. It's very important that the objective is clearly defined while launching each campaign and each step is taken with much caution as the damage caused can be irreparable. The Return on Investment on a Social Media Campaign, unlike that by the usual channels, is not defined over a short period of time, but is more determined from long term perspective. For e.g. The weblink of that innovative ad campaign can be forwarded from one friend to other after a year of the campaign launch and have a positive impact and even a 'sale'.

Social Media Marketing is thus a 'Strategic Investment' and thus calls for a long term vision. There can be manifold uses of an effective social media presence like it can help building a brand image, boost brand recall, help through a sale, keep the existing customers informed about the new products etc. While each company is unique and have their own unique 'positioning' in the market amongst competitors, listed below are some of the recommendations which may help in establishing an effective online presence.

DO's

1) Maintain Messaging Consistency

The first and foremost thing that any corporate should keep in mind that social media is a powerful channel to further your brand reach and should be in conjunction with your brand positioning. A 'messaging consistency' should be maintained across social media websites that are chosen to establish a presence in. This has to be ensured by consistent messaging – for example, the timing and content of a *tweet* should match what's *posted* on the wall of Facebook.

2) Plan well for 'IF, THEN, ELSE' manner

For a corporate, in order to establish a populist presence, it's very important to have a well laid out plan The step wise (IF, THEN, ELSE) plan should be in place in order to understand the user behavior, collect feedback and then iterate. For example, IF the users do not like a new post and give negative comments on the same , THEN analysis should be done and if found justified, the next post should carry a clarification/rectification, ELSE the same picture post should be retained and users comments be dealt with (pacify, explain etc).

3) Prepare for ASAP *'fixing'*

The time available to 'fix a feature/application, page settings etc' which has got negative user response is very less. The 'ASAP' (as soon as possible) generations requires the actions to take place as users react. Thus during the initial launch days 24×7 monitoring of the feedback by the target audience is very important.

4) Customize content adapting to latest trends

Given the continuous 'need for change' of a generation 'spoilt for choice', there is a need of constantly evolving and adapting to the 'latest trend' in order to keep the audience engaged. For e.g. If humorous images/videos are a fad then you may want to add some humour to the campaign. Similarly there is an increasing adoption of 'video on web' due to growing broadband penetration. The target audience's preference need to be studied and the campaign targeted accordingly.

5) Engage the Audience

It's very important to strike a conversation with your audience. For example, if someone asks a query on the 'Wall', the online community manager(s) should be adept at handling it and respond quickly. Also, utmost care should be taken that the response is appropriate and worded correctly.

If you don't respond for a long time (that's more likely to be in minutes or even seconds for today's generation), users lose interest. It's very important to prioritize these responses and give first priority to those that can attract negative publicity/press.

6) Make customers feel good

Ego boosting works the best with this generation as this generation wants everyone to take a note of what they said. Thus applauding people who post something good and informative as a comment to the blog, video or response to your wall posting, can really help attract more people and retain the interest of the audience. Not only the positive, but also constructive criticism should be noted and given due mention. This shows transparency.

7) Use interactive third-party applications

The community members might get monotonous with the same kind of content. These days it is very common for brands to take help of third-party applications, which are later on embedded with the brand's Facebook page. These applications are often prepared with the brand and customer in focus. It could simply be an entertainment application or a purely utility application like a store locator application which could be used by retailers. Many of the conversations with the community manager could be eliminated, if valuable information is made available to the community members through such interactive applications.

Dont' s

1) Don't make it a monologue

Social Media is not about broadcasting information about your brand/firm. It's about communicating. Just a one way flow of information can make it unattractive for the customer who 'likes' your page on Facebook. Given the attention spans of the Gen X, Gen Y and Gen Z who are avid users of Internet and thus the social networking websites, it takes very less time for them to lose interest.

2) Don't ignore negative comments/feedback

Taking criticism positively is a very important proponent to build the brand image. When a user posts something negative, try to first understand what the user is disgruntled with. Interpret the corrective action and if required, immediately intimate the respective team (marketing, sales, operations, human resources etc). Also get the commitment on the time required to resolve the issue and convey it to the user. For example if it's a delay in servicing, first apologize and then convey the time it will take to fix the issue. This will create a positive impression and the customers will start perceiving it as a brand/firm which 'cares'. Social media is about engaging the user and more importantly 'listening' to the voice of the users on a real time basis by way of reading his/her comments on your social media page. This user voice needs to be converted into 'action items' and then acted upon. This honest feedback is very important and sometimes the ideas given by the user can be helpful in the launch of a new product, improving an existing one or improving service quality.

3) Don't post 'updates' unnecessarily

Engaging users by posting updates regularly is a desirable activity. However, posting unnecessarily is not perceived positively. It may not be necessary to post updates about the topics not directly relevant to the brand like political issues etc. This may result in loss of focus and brand erosion in the long term causing customers to lose interest in your social media page.

4) Don't involve in unnecessary arguments on the 'wall'

If by a rational reply or replies to a post by someone on your 'wall', an unnecessary argument is triggered off and/or it appears that the person has an agenda, it's advisable to immediately stop participating (replying further to what he/she posts). If you continue, it may result in heated exchanges causing much more damage to the brand image. One of the best ways to deal with the situation is to intimate openly on the wall that you would like to have a personal communication with this other person who has created this situation. 'To understand the issue better' can be one of the most adept reasons cited for the same. Then you can establish a one-to-one communication and resolve the issue.

5) Don't delete your status update/post

It just takes seconds for your update/post to reach the walls of your hundreds or thousands of followers. So, if you delete a post/ update it doesn't mean it won't reach the wider audience. Hence, if by mistake you have posted/updated wrong information, don't feel shy to apologize in public. Accepting the mistake will garner respect for you. We all make mistakes. It's human. However always remember the golden rule 'Think long enough before posting'. The post/update is like an arrow which is almost impossible to retrieve once shot!

6) Don't concentrate only on selling

It's the 'content' which engages the user and in turn draws attention to your Facebook page. If most of the posts/updates from you are linked only to sales, then the user may lose interest and this can even lead him/her to not be a community member anymore. The mix of content should in such a way that it keeps on attracting the attention of the user (contests, videos, pictures etc) while delivering the key message of the brand.

7) Don't indulge in a conflict with your competitors

You should restrain from posting anything maligning your competitors brand image. Even if a competitor indulges in such behavior, you should avoid it. One of the ways can be to come up with a terse and firm message on your wall that it's against your policy to respond to such campaigns. This will most likely cause your competitor to withdraw as people on social media in India have enough common sense and are well educated to appreciate appropriate behavior.

□

5

HOW LIVES ARE CHANGING ON A PERSONAL BASIS

The so far, yet so near generation

Social media has helped bridge gaps in a phenomenal way. People have come back in touch with their schoolmates, collegemates, ex-colleagues, ex-boyfriends and ex-girlfriends whom they had not heard from for a long time! This powerful medium has helped to re-connect and 'maintain' relationships. This is the one of the most positive impacts of it.

However, a very interesting trend is fast emerging. The frequency of friends 'actually meeting' each other has declined precipitously! 'Personalization' has been re-defined! Earlier (*it may sound medieval*), people used to send cards (paper, not e-cards) to their loved ones. Every year on one's birthday, the postman or the courier handed over a bunch of such cards to the birthday girl's/boy's delight! Times changed and cards were replaced by e-cards. Marking the calendar on the wall was replaced by setting up 'birthday alarms'. The next paradigm shift was the 'mobile revolution'. Call rates dropped astronomically and people just started calling or sending SMSs to wish birthdays. The phenomenal shift came about however with the social media revolution. Birthday reminders are present on your 'home page' of almost any social networking site that you use. Most of the people log in at least once a day to check the 'status updates', 'notifications' and birthdays! People just drop a message on the Facebook 'wall' or 'scrap' on Orkut the birthday message. The number of such 'posts' on your birthday is even treated as a matter of self-esteem by some.

There's a very interesting feature in Orkut called '*Fans'*. You can become a fan of any of your friend. Sometimes people coax and cajole their friends to be their '*Fans'* especially, when they are trying to impress 'someone special'! The 'Testimonial' feature in Orkut , also created waves and it had a very fast 'adaptation' in India. In a society like India where 'references' are very important right from establishing a business to getting married, 'testimonials' was undoubtedly the feature which caught a lot of attention! The Indian user was waking up to the 'Social Image'.

The brains have started getting so wired, that people find it comfortable exchanging messages, writing on walls, scrapping and chatting on social networking sites rather than meeting up in person or for that matter even calling someone. The 'virtual world' is changing reality at a fast pace. You get to know not only all the happenings but also how a friend of yours is feeling on a particular day by just reading his tweets or posts on Facebook. The amount of information exchanged is phenomenal. The pictures of a newly bought car, of a wedding you attended, of a vacation well spent, a corporate dinner and sometimes even very personal ones are shared and commented on frequently. The updates of promotion, change of company, relocation, relationship status – everything gets conveyed 'as it happens'. With so much of information known at the comfort of the home and sitting right in front of the computer or the mobile held in hand, tendency for meeting for that 'chit chat' , gossip and just a cup of coffee may get reduced and in some cases have already started happening. On the other side, you may find some new activity partners like going on a trek , or a marathon or reading club etc on the social network . It's advisable however to crosscheck the authenticity of an unknown person before an offline *rendezvous*. The changing habit of interacting just online is catching up in the Indian context, especially amongst youth-to what extent needs to be seen.

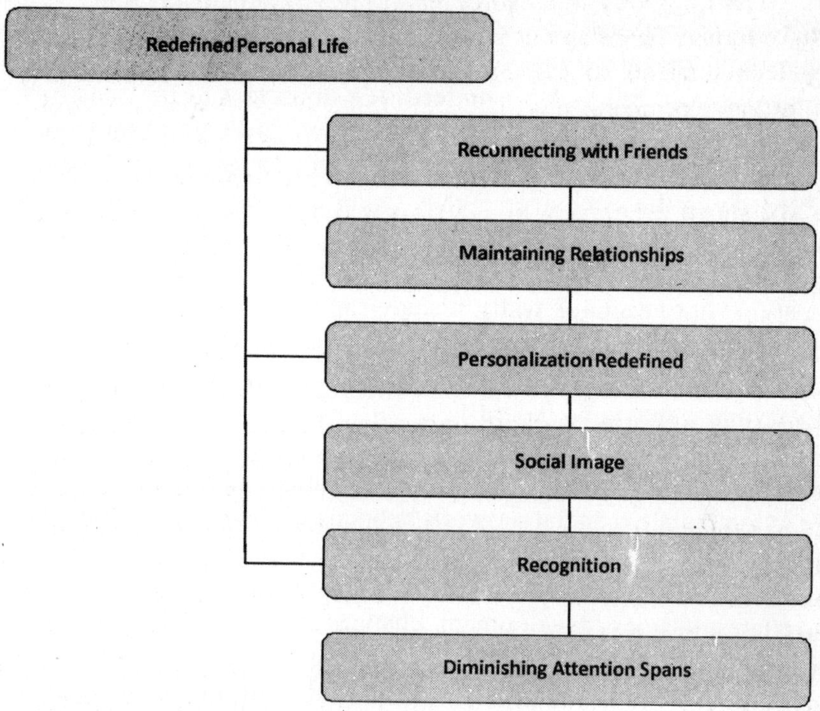

Fig 2: Redefined Personal Life

Recognition is the name of the game

As India has marched ahead to become a 'developed' nation, the confidence levels have gone up in the society. The competition levels have gone up substantially, not only in academics but also in the corporate world. The so called *incentives* need to change to keep a person motivated in a professional environment as an individual marches higher in the Maslow's hierarchy[1] of needs. The need to get 'recognized' is taking preference over monetary gains. Almost everyone wants to '*make a mark*', get noticed and feel important more than ever before.

With the advent of internet on mobiles, people are always '*hooked*' (connected and constantly using) to it- updating status messages, checking updates, commenting on posts at the Facebook wall, responding to tweets etc. People share news, funny videos, pictures of a vacation, quotes, reviews of restaurants and sometimes very personal (break up, job hatred etc) updates! In order to make your presence felt and get noticed, it's important to be 'sensitive' towards what others are sharing too. If you don't 'like' someone's updates or comment on it chances are high that he/she won't bother about doing the same even if they enjoy it or want to express their views on it. If you want people to 'converse' (in the form of *likes* and comments) on your 'stories', (links, videos, pictures etc that you post on your Facebook wall), it's advisable to demonstrate a similar behavior towards them! There's seldom a one-way traffic – Remember that the new media is all about 'conversation' & 'engagement'! Everyone wants to be 'heard'!

The 'conditioning' of a person's status updates based on the reaction from his social network happens in quite a few cases. For instance, if a person did not get any '*like*' or 'comment' or the response has been really lukewarm when his status update was a 'news link' to a latest business development- chances are high that he won't post a similar update again. Humour posts are usually the most sought after ones! Another updates which grabs the most attention is 'relationship status change' e.g. from single to committed or vice versa. Though India is relatively conservative, now the youth are less hesitant in declaring 'in relationship with' < name of the person> even though they are not married! People want their relationship to be recognized by everyone in their social network, much before they get married officially (in traditional manner). On another note this display of 'relationship status', reaffirm the mutual commitment and thus wards away other guys or girls who may be seeking attention of their girlfriend or boyfriend respectively!

Relationships 2.0

Social media is all about 'relationships'. Elaborated in this section are two of the most interesting ones – girlfriend/boyfriend or husband/wife and boss/subordinate. Nowadays, one of the first things that a girl looking for a guy or vice versa does, is to '*check out*' the guy's profile on Facebook or Orkut or any other social networking website. The kind of 'status updates' that you post (e.g. philosophical, funny, silly, religious etc as the perceived by the one who reads it), the photos/videos you share or are tagged in (e.g. party , travel , adventure , family), the 'mutual friend ' list and most important your 'relationship status' (committed, complicated etc) can *'make or break'* the chances of you getting a date! Like in life and more so on the Internet, first impression is the last impression. So if you are looking for someone and/or want to attract some good dates, please make sure that you are uploading the 'right kind of content' suited well to the *type* you are looking for. For instance, if you are 'looking out' for someone who is more outgoing and likes to party, you may find a lot of party photos either shared by him/her or in which he/she is tagged . There may be frequent status updates about '*what happened* 'in the last party, what's the '*dress code'* for the next party and the like.

If already in a relationship, you need to be watchful of the status updates, photos and videos shared on your wall. This is to make sure that your better-half or girlfriend may not get offended by any such posting. For instance a long time friend, in the spirit of the moment, without noticing your relationship status may post something about your ex-girlfriend that may not go well with your current one. In yet another instance, your ex-boyfriend may tag you in a cozy photo which your boyfriend may not like. In India, we are yet far away from the era where most of the parents are also on Facebook/social media – otherwise, one can imagine how worked up the parents wil be on sighting the 'committed' status of their daughter/son. The other school of thought believes in "*I am what I am*" – not a bad approach if the person you seek is also of the same opinion. However, to judge the 'motives of the other', may be a very difficult task!

The other kind of 'relationship' that you need to watch out is 'boss-subordinate'. While most employees would not like to keep the boss as their 'friend' on Facebook, you cannot help it when the boss sends a friend request to you or he/she is a friend's friend and can see your updates! It's always wise to be watchful while posting messages like *'I hate my work' 'What a freaking day'* etc until you are absolutely sure that the boss would not be reading these or a colleague of yours won't be blabbering about these to higher ups! There may be cases where your boss maintains a blog. If he has mentioned the same to you, it may be a good idea to read the same and comment on it. This may do a 'world of good' to your relationship with the boss. On a positive note, who knows the project for which both of you are working may benefit from these 'off-office' 'on-line' discussions!

Diminishing Attention Spans

Cricket is worshipped in India .In every nook and cranny of the country, from grounds to balconies to streets, you can spot kids playing cricket in almost any part of India. There was a time when Test Cricket, played over five days, was the most respected form of the game. Gradually limited-overs cricket, which lasted for a day gathered pace and remained the most popular form of cricket from 80s up until 3-4 years ago. Since then, T20[2] cricket which is a 20 overs a side contest and lasts for 3-4 hours has attained huge popularity in a very short span of time. A T20 cricket world cup is also being organized on a regular basis, since 2007. In India the 'Indian Premier League'[3] has gathered huge TRPs[4]. The matches take place in the evening under flood lights, when people usually return from work. The fan following for the 'shorter version' is not just restricted to cricket. Even on news channels there are short wrap ups, where the entire day is wrapped up in real quick time (5-15 minutes or even less!). The key message that can be derived is that patience levels have diminished significantly. People, especially youngsters now hop and skip jobs with ease compared to the prolonged period of serving the company (sometimes even for a lifetime), which was a common practice followed by their parents. Globalization has helped a huge number of jobs flowing into India, especially from the technology sector and that has helped in a plethora of choices and fast track careers for the younger generation.

The younger generation, especially in the metros, has been highly westernized and now they want everything very fast. The food habits have been changing a lot too and now Indians, especially the working class, prefer eating out just not only on special occasions but almost every weekend. Fast Food chains have spawned all over the country and are growing at a rapid pace with chains like Mc Donalds and KFC[5] increasing their presence not only in Metros but in the relatively smaller cities too.

The trend is not limited to sports and food but has started reflecting on almost all aspects of life. The Gen-X or Y or <whatever it may be named in future> mantra appears to be – fast and new. Everything is wanted as fast as it can be and as new as possible. People get bored browsing through the same websites in a considerably short time. This is posing new challenges not only for social media websites but also for other arenas- education especially being the one of them. Students now need to be taught using content in an 'interactive' and preferably 'video' format. They can get bored flipping pages of their 'age-old' text books especially when they browse at an incredible speed (thanks to broadband) pages on an e-book or watch a video on YouTube.

Life has changed in the Indian context at a phenomenal pace. Taking into account the fact that a huge percentage (~ 46 % as per 2001 Census[6]) of Indian population lies in the age group 15-44, the impact on society is expected to be phenomenal. However another point to be noted is that Internet penetration in India as of Nov'08 was less than 10 %[7].

□

6

HOW SHOULD FIRMS FRAME THEIR SOCIAL MEDIA STRATEGY?

Formulating the social media strategy for any business involves answering quite a few 'whys', 'hows', 'whats' etc. This chapter explores the intermediate decisions to be taken by a firm in its social media journey right from conceptualization of entry to launch.

Why should a firm participate in social media?

Traditional media, as emphasized in this book, is unidirectional in nature. Customers are bombarded with messages from various newspapers, TV channels etc. It is quiet natural for a typical consumer to be exposed to the same brand's message, through the newspaper, radio jingles and the outdoor hoardings. The only mantra that firms earlier seemed to believe was to create a presence wherever possible to ensure that customers were exposed to the message and it helped the 'top of mind recall' for the brand. This probably further helped to generate an intention culminating in purchase of product or service. However, in social media, no matter on how many social media channels a firm creates its presence; it's the end customer who decides whether he/she wants to "follow" the brand on that particular channel. The customer's power to be selective in receiving the message has increased considerably compared to the earlier firm's message broadcasting power. Moreover, the social media industry is also competitive enough, i.e. each social media channel is competing with the other to gain as many unique users as possible. One may relate the social media industry to a TV industry where there are multiple TV channels which can be classified into groups - news, songs, movies, family series, reality shows etc. Each group, more or less broadcasts the same kind of programs targeted to a particular audience with similar interests. Similarly, the various social media channels are offering unique value propositions (like relationships, photos, videos, documents, bookmarks, etc.) which need to be mapped with a firm's objective to go social.

Almost any firm on a given day would be having presence on any one of the traditional media. So the big question a firm needs to answer is "Why should I go for social media, when I am already spending huge money on other media?" If a firm just embarks on a social media campaign because its competitors are doing it, or it's a 'trend' and thus had to be followed, it may lead to a disaster. If this social media strategy is not well thought, it might result in an extremely risky situation. It needs to be clearly understood that unlike other media channels where you can stop advertising or remove banners, any content floated on social media may remain on the web for lifelong. So, even if firms stop using it, people and competitors can dig it somehow and may misuse it, creating problems for the brand.

It's therefore emphasized, that before using social media, firms need to have a clear strategy and a well thought out plan on what are they expecting to achieve through social media. The purpose could be varied – to engage with customers, to source new ideas from customers, to create brand image, to fuel word of mouth of a lesser known brand, to raise funds for a cause etc. Unless a firm has framed its strategy it won't be worthwhile to go with social media.

What are the risks involved?

Customers

It is very common that when firms make a move like launching a new marketing campaign, it creates lot of expectations in the customer's mind. So, it won't be wise to create a social media presence and later on not participate or engage with customers. The fact needs to be realized that a firm won't be able to control all the conversations, which customers have about their brand. Also it wouldn't be always a red carpet welcome for the brands, when they enter social media. It might turn nightmarish, if customers start venting out their anger and their bad experiences with the brand. The firm should be well prepared to tackle customer feedback. There should be a well-framed

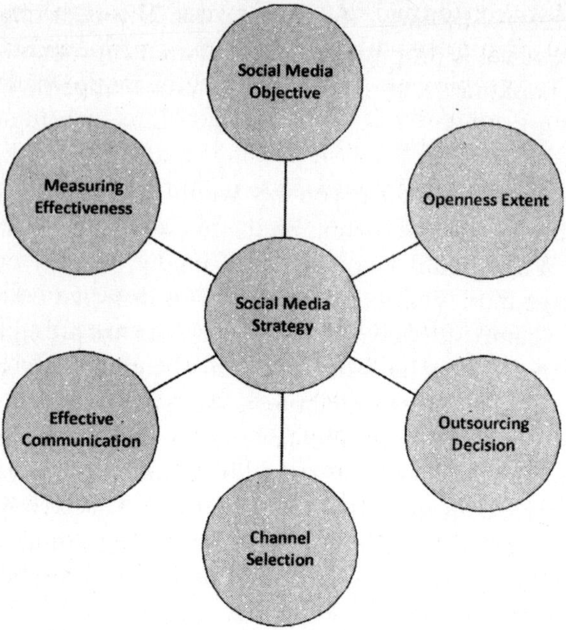

Fig 3: Social Media Strategy

strategy to handle all queries and pacify the customers at the earliest to avoid any further damage. Active engagement should be done to ensure that this risk of not meeting customer expectations is minimized.

Employees

The second source of risk would be internal to the firm – employees. The employees might be either reluctant to support social media, due to their myopic view on social media strategy or might happily adopt it and see it as an entertainment activity rather than professional activity and cause damage to their productivity. The first issue (reluctance) could be easily tackled with adequate and appropriate briefing, but the second issue (performance) needs to be carefully handled. There were times in India (and even today) when employees were not allowed to access their personal email during work hours (in fact they were blocked at servers). Now, the firms need to change their mindset. Some firms might think that only certain people should be allowed access to these social media sites and others not, well on paper it might look a rational decision, however in practice it might create a rift between the two set of employees. This entire phenomenon is dependent on a trust building exercise. A firm needs to trust its employees and employees shouldn't let the firm down. This would take time, but gradually it would be possible to bridge the gap. Sensitizing (by way of briefing/training) and trust building can be the key factors in mitigating this risk.

Support

The customer may pose query on any aspect of the brand – installation, usage, refill, repeat purchase, financing, pending order, promotions etc on the social media channel. The person who is handling the community (commonly known as 'community manager') needs to be connected with every other department. One of the ways in which this entire model can work is a hub and spoke[1] form (as shown in Fig. 4). The double-headed arrows in the figure represent the key aspect of the model. There should be continuous interaction facility between the online community manager and the functional mangers/ departments so that he can extract information at his requirement and use it to engage customers.

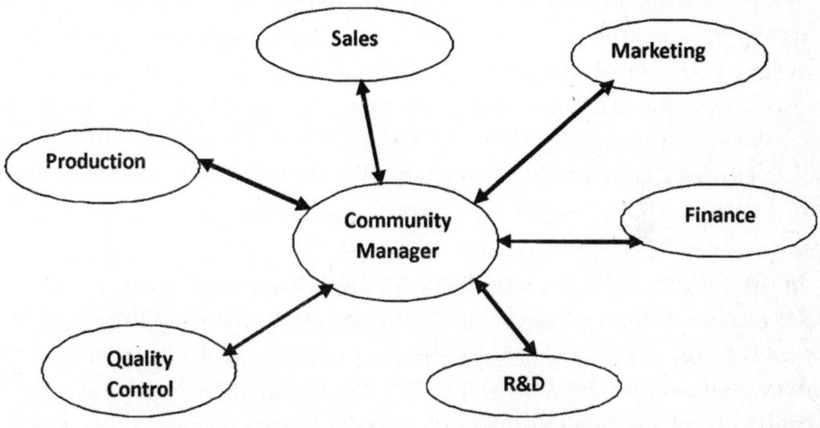

Fig 4: Role of Community Manager

Standard Operating Procedure needs to be worked out while contacting the different departments when needed. This will set a clear chain of communication and ensure the faster and adept response. Also, it will help tackle the odd cases when the online community manager is not clear about which department to contact for a query when a query which involves more than one department. The risk of an inadequate support can thus be tackled by working out the various cases possible and having a process centric approach.

How much should a firm open up?

Firms should be crystal clear about how much information they are going to share about their brand and firm while formulating their social media strategy. A note should be taken of the fact that even competitors might be following your brand closely and monitoring all the conversations you have with your customers. So, when you receive some queries from enthusiastic customers about your new product launches, the firm should decide to what extent the details will be shared. It might be a competitively dangerous move if some information is shared which gives intelligence to your competitor about something (may be a product feature) which your firm wants to keep confidential. In another case, if the firm is small and privately held, some stakeholders might be eager to know about your business model or your performance. You may not disclose the entire information and at the same time, it won't be wise to avoid answering those queries outright. It would require creativity to adequately handle the queries where you cannot share the information and at the same time not let the anger prevail from your customer who raises it. Thus this risk could be addressed by thinking through well about the information that can be shared on an open channel and clear cut instructions need to be given to the online community manager.

Should firm outsource or have an internal team?

This will be a crucial question for many firms. Firms that are outsourcing may cite one of the key reasons as being unaware of how to manage the firm's account on social media. Social media agencies or the professionals or experts in this domain though may have handled just a few brands as extensive social media penetration is relatively new in the Indian context. However, firms need to ensure that they make the right decision. Ideally, firms should have an in-house team to manage their social media activity. This is to ensure that a dedicated pool of resources is continuously working on maintaining firm's social media presence, who develop an in-depth knowledge about the firm's products and services. There is a lot of learning which will take place as time progresses and this dedicated pool will be adept to resolve complicated issues at a faster pace over a period of time.

Even if firms outsource the activity to any agency, firms need to ensure that they have good communication and co-ordination with the agency on a regular basis. The one key aspect of social media communication is the promptness with which the customer is attended. It may happen that when firm's account on social media is handled by an agency, it is actually handled by a community manager who most often handles more than one brand at a time. In such a situation, one of the challenges faced is that the interaction with community members is not an instant activity. It needs to be done on a continuous basis. If a community member poses a query, which the 'multi-tasking' community manager couldn't reply instantly, due to lack of knowledge on that query, it may lead to a dent in brand's image.

The tough part in outsourcing the activity is to maintain 'seamless' communication between the agency and the firm. There are tools available in the market which might assist in the journey, however at the end of the day, only the mother knows better what a child needs and not the day-care aunty! This needs to be realized, sensed by the firm. Firms might think it would be difficult for brand managers to interact with customers when they have other responsibilities to handle. The answer to this would be – change in roles and responsibilities of the brand manager. Probably have an additional brand manager who would maintain the online branding activity, but is in close association with the main brand manager. The risk of mismanaging due to outsourcing is to make sure that the terms and conditions are outlined clearly to the outsourcing firm and the communication process should have well defined SLAs (Service Level Agreement) in place.

Which social media channels should the firm be present on?

Given the hundreds of social media channels presence, it is always going to be a tough choice for firms to decide where to create their presence. However, the key parameters which could be used to reach an optimum decision are listed below:

- ***Deciding their target audience:*** Before deciding on the social media channel, it is important to be clear about the target audience. The social media channel should be suited to the likes and interests of this particular target audience. The social media channel should be popular amongst this target audience and also should be prominent in that part of geography where the firm intends to target. Not all social media channels are used universally. For instance, Linkedin is considered to be very prominent in India[2], while Xing is very popular in countries like Germany, Spain, Portugal[3] etc.. Similarly QQ is a famous social networking channel[4] in China, in spite of the Facebook's dominance across the globe. Next to the geographical presence, firms should evaluate the type of target audience who are member of these channels.

- ***Value proposition*** to be offered by the firm. A simple criterion could be informal vs. formal. Firms should appreciate the fact that certain social media channels do have a very professional image, wherein only formal discussions would yield results and not the informal ones.

- ***Features/positioning of the social media channel:*** Not all social media channels offer range of features. Every channel has its own differentiation and certain key features of engagement are unique to that particular channel. For example videos for YouTube and Vimeo; presentations and documents for Slideshare and Docstoc; short messages (140 characters) for Twitter, photos for Flicksr; music for MySpace etc. Depending on which is a suitable format (mode ,format, length etc) of communication appropriate social media channel needs to be chosen

- ***Content generation process:*** The decision is to determine what type of content could the firm generate on a sustainable basis to ensure sufficient customer engagement? This content could be generated from within the firm or in some instances be sourced from professional content writers. The frequency of the posts should be maintained to keep readers (customers) engaged.

- ***Uniform Messaging:*** It's extremely important to ensure that the consistent message is delivered across all channels. Hence, key features across the prospective social media channels should be identified on which the firm seeks to create presence and modify their content generation accordingly ensuring that the message that the firm wants to deliver is the same across channels and the consumer does not get confused.

What are the key factors in ensuring an effective communication?

With reference to the fact that social media is not a broadcasting medium firms should devote due efforts to listen. In this interaction medium there may be suggestions, complaints, and appreciations about the firm/brand on the social media. Even though the firm may not have presence on any of the social media channels, people on the media may be discussing about their brand/firm. Firms should first try to have a sense of all those conversations and understand on what aspects are customers discussing about their brand. This would help them in positioning their social media strategy. Also, after having created the presence on social media channels, firms should regularly direct efforts towards listening. This could be facilitated with use of various tools available in the market, but should be practiced religiously.

How do I measure effectiveness?

After creating presence on appropriate social media channel, firms would be eager to judge the efficiency of a particular channel. However, judging the efficiency of a particular channel in generating engagement with customers is a tough task. It is not as simple as pagerank or number of hits received in the SEO domain. In this domain, what matters is the extent of engagement a firm is able to build with its customers and more importantly sustain it over a period of time to reap long term results. It is very common in the industry for agencies to charge firms on number of fans/community members accomplished on the brand community, no. of likes received; no. of comments made by community members, no. of times the content was shared further by the community members, no. of times the content was downloaded etc. Agencies use these tangible criteria to pacify firm about their social media efforts. However, firms lose the ultimate target of the social media activity, i.e. 'engagement' and 'connect with the customer'. Social media is a powerful medium to have two-way interaction with the customers and 'positively influencing' them should be the primary output of implementing the Social Media Strategy. *(Read Chapter 7: Social Media ROI for detailed information on how to evaluate the returns from social media activities)*

□

7

SOCIAL MEDIA ROI– MEASURING SUCCESS

In traditional media the main emphasis was on getting the message 'delivered' effectively, and the 'response' was to be measured in the purchase intent and subsequently, the purchase. Some of the metrics which lead to selection of the traditional media for marketing (or to run a particular campaign) are TRPs in TV, Listenership in radio, readership in newspapers and magazines, etc. Firms benchmark their returns vis-à-vis their competitors to judge the effectiveness of a campaign and subsequently return on investment. Broadly, traditionally the companies have been communicating with people for:

- Informing about new products or services or sales offers etc
- Brand building by showcasing innovativeness, corporate social responsibility, superior customer service etc

Now, given the fact that engagement is the main purpose of social media, measuring success becomes all the more complicated. Communication in the real sense of the word is 'interactive' and 'high involvement'. To add to this, the 'word of mouth' has a far wider reach through blogs, reviews and even 'comments on the various posts of the brand as well as its competitors. Another interesting factor is the 'life long' nature of web content. For instance, there may be a case that a brand awareness campaign ran by a firm six months ago, may start fetching results now as the 'viral' ad or video that it created may have taken this time to reach the tipping point. Add to that vast number of social media channels, varied user behavior across these channels, multiple technological features, no industry set format and the problem of measuring 'return' becomes even more complex.

Almost all functions in an organization (Sales, Marketing, PR, R&D, Customer Support, Finance etc) get impacted, directly or indirectly by Social Media. Though, one cannot neglect the tangible returns in business like sales, bottom line, cost efficiency etc., it has to be understood that some of these are a direct outcome of building the base of brand image, positive brand sentiment and word of mouth through 'engagement'. The primary goal should be to increase the effectiveness of each business function by utilizing Social media, which should ultimately reflect in the bottom-line of the company. The main impact, as we see of Social Media is to "influence" a customer (prospective and existing) to be more aware about the brand, trust it and ultimately be a brand advocate. This also remains the key challenge faced with 'measurement' of Social Media ROI as it is extremely difficult to 'measure' influence impact. Consider the case when a customer gets attracted by a Makemytrip.com (MMT), an online travel company, social media campaign about "Cheap Fares", ends up searching the cheapest fair on MMT and finally purchases a ticket from the economy airline company's website rather than MMT. If at the same point of time, this economy airline company is also running a Social Media campaign which is not as effective as MMT, it still may get credited for increase in sales! In another case a user may be on twitter and Facebook, but may get inspired by reading a blog written by someone not related to the company to buy something from the company. The opinion that we have therefore is that at best there can be estimates of the 'influence' and hence the ROI.

There are various new "Calculators" and "balanced scorecards" which have been proposed and some used, in order to measure the "ROI" of Social Media. We recommend a "metrics based approach" which measures the 'influence' effectiveness.

Though a difficult task, it's very important that metrics be measured to judge the effectiveness of the campaign.

1. **Traffic:** Page Views can be a starting point. One should also keep a track record of "Impressions" and then the conversion rate leading to "Click Through" of a particular link if shared by the reader. Also important is to measure the number of

unique visitors to the social media page (Facebook, Twitter etc) . This will help establish, the reach of the site and then on further analysis 'influence' of a particular 'tweet' or a 'post' on Facebook.

2. **Time Spent:** Track the average time spent on your social media page. Keep evolving and changing the interface (background in twitter, layout etc) and observe the delta of time spent (improved or degraded). The User interface plays a very important role in catching the attention of the user, and if the content is good, the user may spend more time exploring the brand.

3. **Comments:** For every tweet or post, you can check how many 'comments' you have got and also monitor the 'positive' or 'negative' reaction to it. This can help you adapt to the way audience perceives and subsequently make your communication style more effective. Usually, videos and pics attract more attention than just plain text. For an emerging economy like India, where the broadband still does not has a wide reach, it has to be an intelligent mix of text/video/pics as the video and pics longer time to download.

4. **Re-tweets/Share:** This can help you gauge the potential 'brand advocates'. This shows that the content is found useful to the extent that the user is ready to share it with his network. Further analysis to determine which kind of audience (professional/housewives etc) is getting attracted towards what kind of 'retweets' etc, can aid the brand in adapting the messaging accordingly.

5. **Downloads:** This could be an indicative metric in case of rich content like presentations, pdf files, videos etc. If the user has gone the distance of downloading the content, this would have happened as the user appreciated the relevance of that content.

6. **Sales:** A particular 'discount' code can be broadcasted by

Twitter, another one for Facebook etc and then it can be tracked which of the sites is leading to 'sales conversion'. This is probably the most tangible and straightforward ROI that can be measured from a Social Media Campaign.

7. **Customer Support Queries:** Time should be tracked from time of posting a query to resolution and level of customer satisfaction. If the number of Customer Support queries is on the increase and the messaging is getting lost in these, a brand should open another page for Customer query resolution.

8. **Social Media Site/Channel Effectiveness:** The above metrics should be analyzed for each of the Social Media sites/channel and checked which of them is more effective in terms of traffic, time spent, conversations, brand advocacy and sales. This will help to learn from the user behaviour which of the sites/channels presence needs to be made more effective.

In this chapter, until now social media ROI aspect has been discussed with the assumption that firm has created its brand community on social media channels and has decided to engage with users on a continuous basis. However, can a firm measure ROI on efforts even before creating brand community on social media? Earlier in this book, it's highlighted that though the firm might not have created community, users still may discuss about it. If a firm which is not present on social media, assess the conversions that were targeted at their brand it may reveal some startling facts about the brand and the perception users have. In this case the firm is not participating and interacting directly with the customer, but firm is monitoring the conversations targeted at the brand from behind the screen, which is termed as *Listening* in the social media industry. This listening exercise should help firm in deciding the future course of social media strategy. The 'Return on listening' is surely the invaluable insights about the brand.

It's important to understand that what attracts a individual to social media mostly are the personal objectives like finding old friends, converse with their friends, find new friends, etc. Apart from these, social media channels provide lot of features like social gaming, chat, contests, etc. to entertain users. Taking this into account, the time available with user to pay attention to your brand is considerably less. The 'content' is what can attract him/her to your brand and thus getting the 'content strategy' tailored to your target audience is critical to success. Once you attract the user to *'like'* your Facebook page or become follower of a brand community, he/she enters into a 'psychological contract' with the brand for receiving messages and getting some benefit from the brand community. If the brand fails to offer that expected benefit, no matter how good your offline offerings are, there is high chance that 'psychological contract breach' online might spill over to the offline world. So, brands cannot afford to disappoint their brand community users. Feedback needs to be collected from the customers/users on a continuous basis to ensure that the use of Social Media channels/sites is effective and is keeping the pace with the ever changing needs of the users. Also on a regular basis, the new channels/sites should be evaluated to ensure a presence there. Besides tracking the metrics for self, a brand should also do the same for it's competitors. The best practices should then be adapted to its social media presence.

□

8

SOCIAL MEDIA UTILITY BEYOND BUSINESS

In the past one required to be a great politician, businessman, academician, sportsperson, scientist, philosopher, artist, or in worst case a terrorist to be well-known across the globe. Why wasn't a common man getting attention? This can be attributed largely to the business model with which media businesses were traditionally run. Media thrived on the number of eyeballs (number of people who were exposed to a particular media channel) they could manage, and these eyeballs were dependent on the 'mass' popularity of the content that these media channels broadcasted. This made channels to focus primarily on the content that could be of prime importance for catching attention for all of or at least a majority of their target audience. In the process, common person was seldom covered by the media, until he/she could '*make it big*'.

In the present times, where preferences are highly differentiated, content that can be of prime importance to one may not be even remotely important to the other, absolutely irrelevant to the third and so on. This may happen even if they are perceived as having a 'similar' demographic profile. Similarly the format in which the content is delivered, may find different preferences amongst different people. Social Media can cater to the varied preferences in a much more cost effective manner. Further, the ease of accessing content at one's convenience can be facilitated with a relative ease as compared to traditional media (newspapers, TV channels etc)

The fundamental purpose of any media is to facilitate communication. The form, intensity and convenience of communicating message might differ with reference to the technology used. This message that needs to be communicated may have varied purposes – news, cultural events, college admission, fair happening in the city, health camp, marriage invitation, weather forecasts etc. All these messages however can be communicated using one single medium (e.g.: newspaper), instead of having separate medium designated for different purposes. Similarly, the myth that social media is useful only for making friends and branding business, should be done away with. In this chapter are exhibited the various purposes for which social media could be used and also an attempt has been made to explain how one may use various social media channels to ensure effective reach of message.

Personal recognition and branding

We Indians have an inherent need of getting noticed and recognized amongst our near and dear ones. If we can gain recognition amongst people outside our 'circle of trust' and especially the global audience, this really can boost self esteem. Social media has empowered every individual with even simplest of the talent to gain popularity through this amazing media. MySpace was the pioneer social networking website which empowered every individual to exhibit his/her talent. Any individual who could compose music had an opportunity to upload the composition on MySpace and sharing with friends, who further shared with their friends. This gave the person an opportunity to create a brand of himself/herself, without taking help of the traditional media. More importantly, one could do these things free of cost, and gain fame for which celebrities sometimes spend millions. MySpace facilitated broadcasting music and video files, but how about an emerging chef, a painter, a photographer, an educationist, a technologist or a lawyer for that matter. There are millions of them across the globe, but given the cut-throat competition not everyone can make it big through the traditional route. However, they can definitely use appropriate social media tools to gain recognition in their field and build their brand.

A photographer can use Flickr, a photograph sharing social media channel by Yahoo. With the increasing penetration of mobile phone, iPhone etc. anyone with keen interest in photography can capture the real-life interesting experiences and share it with the world out there at ease and almost free of cost. There is high probability of someone with the common interest to find you and get in touch. Think of millions of people viewing your photography, without organizing an exhibition, and you might make it big one day as people take notice.

A technologist or a lawyer can share their knowledge through blogs. Blogs are extended notes wherein one can express his/her ideas without the limitation of space (as it is a constraint across some form of social networking channels). These blog posts when later shared on their Facebook, Twitter, Linkedin accounts can result in a viral, where their friends may share this post in their own network and the chain may further get extended. For blogs to become search-engine friendly, one should use key tags, so that they appear higher on search results. Blog posts need to be posted at regular interval of time, as people expect steady and more information from you once they get interested in your blog.

Similarly, a chef need not wait for a '*Master Chef*' event to be organized and doesn't need to depend on luck to be shortlisted. If you are eager to share the recipe, just take help of a handycam or a decent mobile phone and record the video of yourself preparing a dish. Then upload it on YouTube, which is a videosharing social networking channel owned by Google. You may share it with your friends and the viral effect can draw many to your channel. You have high chances then of getting popular and who knows, getting a professional to notice you!

If you are an automobile expert and fond of automobiles, share your reviews on new automobiles (cars, bikes etc) through social media. After you visit auto expos, you may be so *charged up* to share your experience with someone who can benefit and appreciate your inputs. Writing a blog post and sharing it on your Facebook or Twitter account can be the easiest way to reach out. In this way you can build your 'auto-expert' brand. This also applies to technology geeks who review appliances etc. You could post your reviews on latest electronic devices, mobile phones, computer peripherals, software, games etc. People are always on the lookout for some 'expert opinion' before making such a purchase. The demand of such inputs and reviews is never ending. It all depends on how well you can utilize social media to gain popularity and be regarded as an expert.

People from all walks of life have already started to build their own 'brand' using social media, no matter which city they come from. The continuous inputs that you will get from the readers on your expertise will also help you hone your talent further and become a professional!

Raising funds for a cause

There are many volunteers, activists and organizations (including non-profit, non-governemnt organizations) around who are trying their best to contribute for the well-being of underprivileged people. However, they need enough funds to sustain these activities on a longer term. Many of these depend on their personal network and the word of mouth to attract funds, as they don't have enough funds to express their cause and raise funds through traditional media (publishing an advertisement in a newspaper etc). Social media could be a great resource for these organizations. If you are an independent person working for a cause or a NGO, you should establish your presence on social media and express in detail all activities that you are doing for the betterment of the society. You could share photographs, insights from beneficiaries to express your commitment in a better manner. The wider reach of social media would substantially increases the chances of spreading the word.

Solving criminal cases

You may have read in newspapers that criminal cases were solved using proof from social media. We are not sure if Indian Penal Code acknowledges the content from social media as proof, but definitely in the western world this has now been an accepted practice[1]. Social media allows an individual to express oneself. So, be it happy or sad moment, an individual usually is in a hurry to express his/her feelings with the network of people around him/her. Unknowingly every one of us is creating a biography of our life on social media. It could be dangerous to share *everything* about your life, as some of your rivals (business or otherwise) may use this to create an opportunity to harm you.

Crowdsourcing[2]

A lot of us (the young generation) have grown up using 'Yahoo Answers' for even simplest of queries we had in our life. At http://answers.yahoo.com/(URL for Yahoo Answers), anyone can raise a question and can answer any question about any topic[3]. About everything in our life we want to have more information e.g. finding a good hotel to stay in an unknown city, a travel suggestion, finding a good apparel store, finding a cutting-edge technology product. We have evolved in the way that no longer we look forward to guidance only from our parents, relatives or close friends. We are in need of best available guidance, and hence open to listen to anyone who has the best information. It would be so cumbersome for us to first identify whom to ask. After arriving at a list of people, people usually had to mail or call each of them regarding the query and wait for them to answer. With the advent of social media and its increasing adaptation, one can now just post a query only once on his/her profile page and it would be reflected on the 'wall' of all friends one has on his/her social network. The process has simplified and the reach has increased to a great extent. In least possible time one can get information from as many people as possible, which is often referred to as "crowdsourcing". In business contexts, firms use this to design new products, modify existing products/services, to get new ideas on advertising concepts, to frame slogans for their brands etc. from the '*crowd*' (people in the social network)

Event Marketing

If you are organizing any event, even if it is a small informal get-together party amongst your friends, it's very convenient to organize it using social media. Facebook and LinkedIn for example offer the feature "Events" where in you can mention the name of event, purpose of the event, location, timing etc. As soon as you create this event page, it will be reflected in the feeds of your friends and they would be informed. Anyone who has suggestion regarding change in location or time would post the comment on that page, which again would be reflected to everyone. In Facebook, this event page offers a RSVP feature wherein, there are three alternatives – Yes, No and Maybe[4]. As your friends click on any of those, you can easily plan the logistics for the event depending on expected participation. If this is a public event (where anyone can be invited), chances are high that it can go viral and reach many more than in your personal network. When any of your friends clicks on the "Yes" button this message is reflected on all his/her friend's feed and now they all get to know about the event, without your efforts to inform them. So, your event gets much higher visibility than, you can manage just on your own. The topic of discussion, menu, timing etc and other details related to the event could be finalized using this event page. The attendees could get to know each other even before attending the event. This helps in breaking the ice before the event and hence during the event you could easily converse with each other more effectively.

Above listed is a 'sample' of ways in which Social Media is impacting different areas of life for good. There are numerous other ways in which people have received help over the network and benefited. The idea is to keep thinking how to use the social network and evolve to use it for your maximum benefit.

□

9

SOCIAL MEDIA INFLUENCE & OPPORTUNITIES

Social Media is influencing almost all aspects of life, beyond networking. The way people work in different areas has undergone a significant change due to the advent of the new media. In many ways the 'ways of working' across fields have got influenced. Listed below is a sample to put things into perspective.

Journalism

Almost all the news channels, print media etc., are present on the social media. The social network to start with has become a vital source of information, which cannot be neglected. The journalist of course needs to filter out the noise to get some inputs which he/she can pursue. This monitoring has to be done in real time as sometimes it can give the vital edge and the channel/newspaper may be the first one to cover the story. Even for a community (religions, cities etc), there are websites, Facebook pages etc. A journalist can log on to these and search if there is an issue/concern facing a particular community and being raised by someone on the forum (Facebook page/Twitter handle etc). If this is validated and pursued, it can surely enhance the brand image of the journalist along with newspaper/ channel in that particular community and also amongst others. The whole world of journalism has to keep a close watch on the "News Feed" in Facebook, or "timeline" in Twitter as they can hold precious cues to get a 'hot' story! As it is not possible for the journalist to be active and all ears for such important information, online community managers have a vital role to play and relay relevant information to each journalist which can then be followed up by him/her.

Recruitment

It's always a cumbersome task for an employer to cross-check the information about the prospective employee. The employers always have the risk of trusting the incorrect information presented by prospects. It's also difficult to judge the character. Today, social media can facilitate removing 'information asymmetry' amongst the recruiters and prospects to a large extent. Recruiters these days are increasingly using social media to gather more information about the prospective employees. It's difficult for anyone to cheat your accomplices consistently as the 'social image' can be very well reflected by the individual's participation in the social media. Recruiters can easily understand and know more about a person by scanning social media channels and his/her behaviour on them. The kind of posts you make, kind of comments you post, kind of photographs you share, kind of content you like across online media, exhibits your social graph and conveys a lot beyond the two or three page CV. For example, if you have applied for some position which demands creativity, and you have a related blog/Flickr channel/YouTube channel where you have relevantly expressed yourself, you would be perceived as a genuine creative person, rather than just having stated it on the CV. This enhances the credibility of the candidate and increases the probability of being recruited.

Job postings on a company's online community can help save time and cut down on costs. The general queries can be solved in discussion forums. Career blogs can be another effective medium for such openings. Further, the employees should be encouraged to share it with their friends by posting the new openings on their profiles. Some of the 'head hunting' gets done when the HRs send 'friend requests' to the prospective professional. This is not very professional and if the HR finds the person a perfect fit, a private message can be sent explaining the context.

Marketing

The marketing function can do the activity that's very critical to a brand's success much better than ever before. It can now 'listen' in much more effective manner. It's listening which helps identify the 'needs' and thus some wonderful products take shape. Nowadays, people blog about both good and bad experiences, some of them related to products and services. People also leave comments on a company's blog giving feedback and interact with the company on Twitter, Facebook etc. The feedback is real-time and so has to be the 'need assessment'. Marketers though still rely to a large extent on surveys but 'Social Media Analytics' has also got an increasingly important role to play in the decision making – whether it be about a product conceptualization or campaign. Also an increasing amount of budget is now allocated to online advertising especially in developed countries. In India also, social media presence is becoming more of a norm than a differentiator – some of which is outlined in the case studies chapter of the book. *(Chapter 10)*

Politics

Door to door campaigns may be the norm for political campaigns for the earlier generations, but Gen Y's mind share can be grabbed through the social media. In some developed countries the time spent on Facebook is now comparable to the time spend watching TV[7]. The elections in some developed countries have already noticed the influence of Social media. In the developing countries where the internet penetration is much less, the impact is still going to be big as the educated people are the opinion leaders usually in any society. Even in India, the mainstream parties like BJP do maintain their Facebook page.

The social media revolution has opened up a lot of opportunities for both professionals as well as entrepreneurs. Here are some examples:

Application Development

Apart from the technical (web development/enhancement) for social media sites, applications (App) development has also created a sizeable industry where specific (web) 'applications' are developed either for enhancing a corporate brand image, or just for fun purpose/ getting user attention to some other site or in a some cases to monetize using advertising revenue from these. The conceptualization of the App involves a lot of creativity in order to catch the audience's attention. The competition is tough with numerous apps available in Facebook and other social networking websites. The App much like

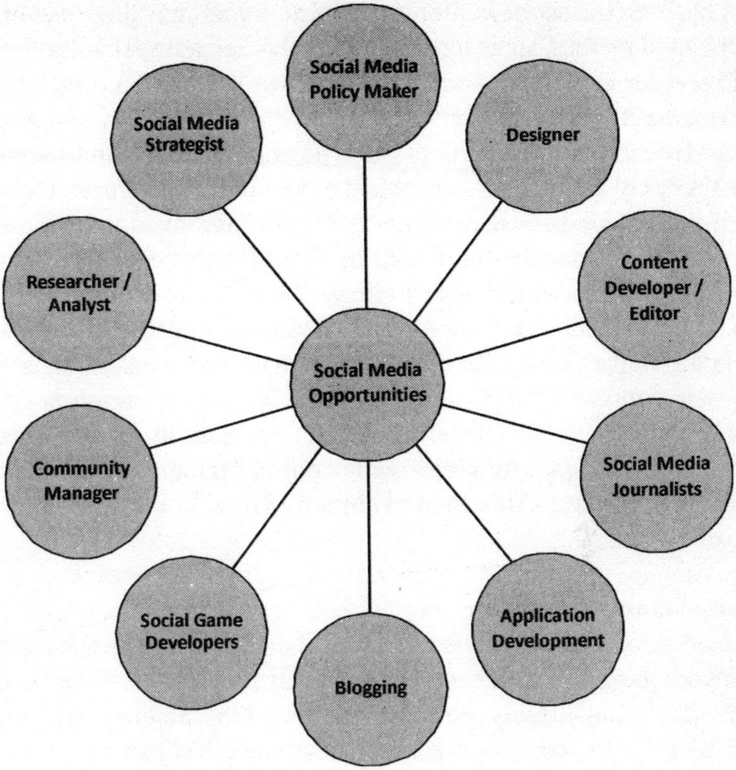

Fig. 5: Social Media Opportunities

any other social media interface/channel needs to continue re-inventing itself in order to sustain audience attention. Due to an increasing number of people not only in developed, but also in developing countries, beginning to access Social Media on the mobile, a whole new industry is being spawned for 'mobile compatibility' of these Apps and also exclusive mobile Apps. In 2009, the global market of mobile applications was worth 1.7 billion USD according to Research2guidance[1].

Blogging

There are quite a few examples in Indian as well as global context, where what started as a blog, developed to full-fledged websites and now have numerous hits per day. There are quite a few niche audiences for different kind of contents, for e.g., some may like technology content in general, some technology content related to cloud computing only, some technology content related to new media, and so forth. There are broad based themes around which blogs have also become popular e.g.: movies, humour etc. The monetization can be achieved by means of Google Ad-sense[2] and other similar programs. Once you apply for the Ad-sense program and it gets approved by Google, ads on your blog start being placed by Google. You can get paid when someone clicks on the ads or views[3] them. It can range from a cent to dollars per click depending on what kind of 'targeted' advertisement is being displayed on your blog. There can be more models like offering a basic content for free and charging a fee for the premium content on your blog to the readers. Besides, revenue in monetary terms, quite a few people use blogging for popularizing their views and/or products/services. This then eventually leads to monetary gains by means of sales.

Social Gaming Developers

Social Gaming refers to games played on a browser with social network integration[4] element and is usually multiplayer. Social Gaming despite being hugely popular still remains at large not tapped monetarily. Social network game developer companies range from well established (like Zynga[5]) to start ups. The mobile compatibility of these games will be a future focus area and the biggest challenge remains monetization. According to e-marketer[6], a research group Social Gaming Market will surpass $ 1 bn in 2011.

Apart from the Technical Development related, listed below are some of the other key profiles which have emerged as a result of Social Media. The roles and responsibilities of these profiles vary significantly according to each company/industry. Below descriptions are 'broad based':

Online Community Manager (CM)

This person manages the 'virtual face' of the brand across multiple social media sites (Twitter, Linkedin, Facebook etc). The job entails moderating the community, monitoring discussions, checking spam and actively engaging the audience through interactions. The CM is also expected to pass on the relevant information (e.g. a customer grievance tweet, post about a good idea on the Facebook wall etc) to the respective department and monitor a 'closure' for the same. CM is a customer advocate and should check that the customer's best interests are not compromised. At the same point of time, CM has to play the role of a brand evangelist by 'influencing' rather than 'persuading' the community members. He/she should be passionate about the brand and the community around it. Ideally, the person needs to be connected with the brand's community round the clock; however he/she could make use of some social media dashboard tools to simplify one's tasks.

Social Media Researcher/Analyst

This person is involved in studying the competitors' strategy, analyzing data to understand trends & issues. For instance which channels (sites/channels) are being the most effective, customer satisfaction pertaining to query resolution, interaction, ROI etc. This individual should be well-versed with various analytics tools available in the market, should have both analytical and behavioural bent of mind. Insights need to be generated not just on analytics, but also behavioural aspects, to understand why community members behave in a particular manner.

The Social Media Strategist

This person is expected to take the analysis as an input and determine the future roadmap and strategy for the brand(s). Any individual who has had sufficient experience in the digital media marketing, with adequate knowledge of social media would fit into this position. The person would be responsible for every aspect of the social media strategy right from setting objectives, selecting right people, selecting right social media channels, communicating the strategy to internal members (and to agencies, if the activity is outsourced), measuring RoI etc. An ideal person would be one who has the ability to keep himself/herself updated with new technological developments in the field and assessing its effectiveness for the given social media objective of the brand. So basically, he/she needs to be both tech savvy and customer-centric.

Social Media Policy Maker

Ideally should be a person with knowledge of cyber laws in general and in-depth knowledge of the uses/misuses social media. His/her responsibilities would include framing social media policy for the organization, communicating the same to the concerned employees, arranging social media training sessions for employees who are not well versed with it etc. Social media policy maker is responsible to ensure social media activities are conducted in an ethical manner, and no harm is caused either to brand or the organization by the employees involved in the activity.

Designer

User interface plays a key role Social Media. "First impression is the last impression" is most pronounced as far as Internet and more so social media websites go. If the design is not 'keeping pace' with the times, it may spell a doom for the portal/channel no matter how superior its features are compared to its peers. Another interesting thing is that this generation gets bored very fast and is constantly seeking change. The User Interface (UI) or the design is no different. The designer needs to first understand the voice of customer and then create a design around it. Constantly, this design needs to keep evolving to maintain novelty and also to match the ever changing preferences of the target audience. As the design is the 'door' to the social media experience, designer developing this user interface has a very key role to play. He/she needs to be ably supported by analytics team who give inputs about the user psychology, needs and preferences.

Content Developers and Content Editors

No matter, how relevant or informative the content, presentation (format, structure) holds the key for grabbing the audience attention. The content developers/editors are expected to edit the language and readability of the content to make sure it conveys the message and is not only 'liked' (both in the usual sense and also in the Facebook 'like') but shared by the readers in their social network as well. In general, these content developers should understand the industry in which the brand is positioned, the usual consumer expectations about the product category, for what the brand stands for, etc. Any individual who is good at language and can express the message in an innovative manner wouldn't be sufficient, if he/ she lacked the basic product and brand understanding. Any day, firms would be ready to provide training on certain aspects, but a basic knowledge about the domain would be a prerequisite and help to gain an edge over other candidates.

Social Media Journalists

These can either be full time or hired on a part time basis depending on the need. They promote any event - conference, industry meets, etc for the company by making use of various social media channels/portals like Facebook, Twitter, YouTube etc. They even work with these websites to come up with new ways of using the channels/ portals to suit the need of the audiences. They make sure that the content (text, photos, videos) generated for the event has to be viral in nature, keeping in mind the ethics/values/preferences of the audience.

On the whole the impact of social media is being felt across almost all walks of life and in all fields in developed countries. This will take shape of a Global phenomenon once the internet penetration begins to increase in developing countries like India. When that happens, it can be said that those who will spend time in understanding and putting the social media to its best use, will emerge as winners. □

10

CASE STUDIES

As the book concludes, it's suggested that you introspect and ponder how much more do you know about social media than before having started reading this book? Has your perspective widened about the usage of this new media? During the course of the chapters, simplifying this domain and sharing insights should have exposed you to some key elements of this industry. Much like other media planning activities, social media marketing too starts with a clear objective and well defined strategy before any other tactical steps. The major social media channels which can be used by brands to establish their social media presence have to be utilized judiciously. Certain do's and don'ts should always be considered before making any social media interaction. The trick of the trade lies in generating the right type of content, for the right type of the audience, on the right type of the social media channel. As a logical conclusion, to understand how this domain knowledge is being implemented in real life, this chapter consists of case studies of brands operational in India that have leveraged social media. An honest attempt has been made to present the facts as seen and leave the interpretation of effectiveness of particular brand's social media presence to the reader. After you read through these case studies, you should figure out the best social media strategy for your brand, taking into consideration the industry you belong to. Also you should ponder on the type of brand image you would like to exhibit and the purpose (objective) for which you would like to adopt social media. Even if you are not a professional, you can analyze how different brands position themselves and implement their social media presence. The case studies have been collated from diverse industries for a wide understanding and analyzing some 'common best practices' for a particular industry if any.

At the end of each chapter Key Insights and Observations section shares some of the key takeaways. It has been ensured that key takeaways mentioned in each chapter are distinct and they don't get repeated to the extent possible. Key takeaways from all case study chapters should be analyzed to get a comprehensive understanding of managing brand community on social media channels.

Disclaimers

- The selection of case studies in each product category has been at random choice.
- It is clarified that it doesn't imply that brands which were not included in a particular product category are performing to low standards on social media. An attempt has been made to include brands that would be familiar to most of the readers as perceived by the authors.
- Analysis of the content, that brand has posted on various social media channels for the last few months, has been done. Attempt has been made to conjecture the social media strategy behind the brand on the basis of the same. This is subjective and it may vary from person to person, and hence the viewpoints expressed are authors' interpretation and may not exactly reveal the social media strategy as planned by the firm or brand.
- Please note the date of the data collected in these case studies. As the Social Media channels (Twitter, Facebook accounts etc) are evolving by the minute, there may be changes.
- In some cases there is an explicit mention "when this case study was written". Even when it's not there, please note that every data in any case study like number of fans, photos, video etc is as seen by the authors on the date when that case study was authored.
- The Administrators of the Facebook Pages are often referred to as "*Community Managers*" and the people who *like* the Facebook page or follow a Twitter handle are referred to as "*Community Members.*"
- Social media initiatives of some brands included in this book are managed by social media agencies, while some brands handle them in-house. As it is difficult to share with confidence

which brands are being managed by social media agency, we haven't shared this information.

- These case studies are mere exhibition of facts, authors don't intend to comment on the strategies or tactics followed by the brands, as interpretations in this domain are very subjective in nature.
- The enlisting of social media presence by brands might not be exhaustive, in which case we regret for missing some of the social media channels on which brands might have their presence and it should not be considered intentional.

Note: *Some extensive disclaimers are put in place to ensure that you approach these case studies with an open mind and have an independent interpretation of the facts. Especially, given the nascent state of the industry, it would be difficult for anyone to call themselves experts in the field and thus the authors of this book should be treated as observers.*

10 A. Telecom Service Providers (*Dated: 20th December, 2010*)

Parameters	*Airtel*	*Vodafone*	*Idea*
Social media widgets provided on homepage	Yes	Yes	Yes
Social media presence	Facebook Orkut, Twitter YouTube	Facebook Twitter	Facebook Twitter YouTube
Facebook			
Welcome Fan tab	No	No	No
Info tab details	Yes	Yes	Yes
Integration with other social media tools	No	No	Yes
Community members can make post/ upload photos, videos	Yes	No	Yes
Applications	'3G'	'Delights' 'Regional' 'Promotions' 'Campaigns'	'Idea Language'
Twitter			
Company name	Yes	Yes	Yes
Background image relevant to product	Yes	Yes	Yes
Location	No	No	No
Web address	Home website	Home website	No
Informative bio	Yes	Yes	No
YouTube			
About company	Yes	—	Yes
Video themes	• Videos by users • CXO interviews on TV channels • TV commercials	—	• Videos by users • TV commercials • Snippets of live events sponsored by Idea

Mobile service providers in India are fighting fiercely with each other to gain as much market share as possible. These service providers are trying hard to maintain their brand presence in customer's mind with various promotional activities at regular intervals of time. They engage in various online and offline activities to attract attention of customers. In this industry as the exit barriers for customers are very low, there are high chances of customers switching operators. Moreover, now that number portability has been introduced in India the competitive pressure in this industry is set to rise to a whole different level. In that scenario it would be essential for brands to sustain brand loyalty and maintain the positive brand attitude amongst the customers. Also, it would be necessary for brands to continuously listen to all grievances and make efforts to address them in real-time. In this section, three of the major players in the Telecom services industry are analyzed to access how they were leveraging social media to further their presence in the customer's mind.

AIRTEL *(Case Study no. 1)*

Facebook

The first noticeable element of the Airtel Facebook page was its attractive new logo after Airtel rebranded itself in December, 2010[1]. The username of the Facebook page "Airtel_IN"[2] probably indicated that Airtel would have country specific Facebook pages in the future. Airtel mainly used Facebook page to promote its various products and services other than the mobile services. The products and services that were promoted often were DTH, broadband, Airtel LearnNext, 3G etc. However, the promotion message (post *on the Facebook wall*) was not very straightforward, but conveyed the message in an innovative manner. Current affairs like cricket match that was going on, movie that was to be released, etc were included in the promotional message to grab attention. For example, a post on the wall read:

"Hey guys, India Vs SA is about to start... hope you have subscribed to Ten cricket**. http://p1n.in/topup"** [3]

The URL directed the user to webpage that had information on subscription packs of Airtel Digital TV. In order to keep the community members (those who did *like* the Airtel Facebook page and thus received updates on their wall) engaged otherwise also, Airtel posted updates asking for their prediction of the match results. This evoked a good response from the community members. Another update which grabs substantial attention is the contests. For example:a contest run by Airtel, where it posted a status update on it's wall inviting community members to complete a slogan.

Airtel's Facebook page had an application "3G"[4] where an image was placed with the message *"Enter the world of 3G"* and a click-through tab *"Know more about 3G"* was placed at the bottom right corner of the image. The tab redirected the user to the Airtel webpage where details on 3G services were available. Airtel's emphasis on 3G promotion as compared to it's other products as services could be realized as it has created a special *application* on its Facebook page for the same.

Twitter

Similar to its Facebook page the Airtel Twitter handle was @airtel_in[5] and the logic of having a country specific handle would apply here too. The background image of the Twitter handle matched the visual identity of Airtel logo. The background was in red colour with the inclusion of the new logo.

The following detailed bio was provided—

"India's leading telecommunications company Airtel offers mobile, fixed line, broadband, DTH and enterprise services solutions. Visit our website for more info"[6]

There was a tweet wherein @Airtel_In specifically advised followers to direct all customer grievances and support queries to @Airtel_Presence (Airtel's other Twitter handle). @Airtel_In was primarily used to promote products. Some of the tweets were similar to that of wall posts on the Facebook page. A community member, who might be following the brand on both Facebook & Twitter, might get annoyed with the same message directed to him from various channels. This would be similar to watching the same TV commercial on different channels. Brands need to work with an assumption that there is high chance that the same user might be following the brand on multiple channels. It is quite plausible that the user is expecting something different from various channels and not the same message across channels. The value proposition needs to be differentiated across channels.

Airtel had another Twitter handle - @airtel_presence[7]. However, the Twitter widget placed on the Airtel home website directed to @airtel_In. It could be beneficial to keep conversations on grievances separate from that of promotional conversations, however then it needs to be clearly mentioned on the website. @airtel_presence was a Twitter verified account. This handle addressed queries from customers on mobile services, landline services, broadband connections and DTH services. Anyone who contacted Airtel through @airtel_presence the follower was asked to email the details to airtelpresence@airtel.in for further actions. The tweets on this handle indicated that many followers of this Twitter handle benefited from it and Airtel responded promptly to their queries.

YouTube

Airtel created its YouTube channel on August 18, 2010 and was named as INAirtel[8]. The broad themes of videos uploaded on this channel were—

- Videos by users regarding their experience with the Airtel service,
- Interviews of Airtel CXOs by TV channels,
- Airtel TV commercials.

As and when this chapter was written, Airtel had uploaded 45 videos, the channel had 171 subscribers, and total views of uploaded videos was 405, 238[9]. The purpose of creating a YouTube channel appeared to create a positive image about the brand in the customer's mind. The motive of sharing user experiences was an interesting move, instead of brand speaking about itself. However, videos from YouTube channel were neither shared on Facebook page nor on Twitter handle. This showed lack of integration of the YouTube channel with Facebook page. Also in the current context, where the inclination towards watching videos had increased manifold, this channel needed to be further publicized to increase its popularity which will in turn get an increased mindshare for the customers.

VODAFONE *(Case Study no. 2)*

Facebook

The Facebook page of Vodafone named as *Vodafone Essar, India*[10] served multiple purposes—promotion of products, customer service and a place to handle customer grievances. Vodafone's Facebook page did not have permission for community members to comment or make wall posts. So, Vodafone published posts and community members could only comment on it. The wall posts were very informative with the link which took the user to the "Notes" section where the short description about the offer was available. The community members could interact in this section for further clarification. The posts had an attractive picture icon.

Generally the links shared on the wall of the Facebook page did not redirect the user to the Vodafone website. On clicking the links further information was provided in the *Notes* section of the Facebook page itself.

Four important and innovative tabs were created on the page which provided complete customer service– "Delights", "Regional", "Promotions" and "Campaigns". "Delights"[11] was the special deals service that Vodafone offered. Community members could gain information about the service from this tab. The "Regional" application informed community members about the latest offers available in a particular region. This tab had a user-friendly drop-down menu with all major circles mentioned, so a community member could just select the region from where he/she was based and could know the latest promotions available in that region. This type of customized information is generally provided on the website of any company. The "Promotions"[12] application had all information about the various promotional schemes. When a user clicked on any of the promotions, it took the user to Vodafone website for further information. The "Campaigns"[13] application had some brief information on Vodafone "Magic Box" service, which included – additional benefits, online recharging facility, caller tunes and Vodafone Live. A user interested in any of the above services could click and he/she would be taken to the website wherein the transaction could be completed.

Though community members could not post on the wall due to the settings done by Vodafone, they could voice their concerns at the "Discussions"[14] section of the Facebook page. It was noticed that community members were aware of this feature and it was being used judiciously. As and when this chapter was written there were 406 discussion topics initiated by the community members and Vodafone replied to each one of them. This strategy distinguished the discussions on the same channel.

In the "Campaigns" application there was information for users to join the *Zoozoo* Facebook page. Vodafone leveraged the enormous brand equity of *Zoozoo*. They created a distinct Facebook page for it where Zoozoo TV commercials were shared. Apart from TV commercials they also promoted various contests, games based on *Zoozoo*. The Zoozoo page has not been reviewed extensively beyond this point in this section in order to maintain focus.

Twitter

The Twitter handle of Vodafone, India was @VodafoneIN[15]. The background image of the Twitter handle had Pug placed on the left hand side of the timeline. Vodafone leveraged well both of its icons – Zoozoo (in Facebook page) and Pug. It could be deciphered that the strategy to connect between the brand and the customers and the strong association between its icons with the customers was being adopted. Vodafone had a detailed bio with a very straightforward message – *"Tweet us if you have Queries on your Vodafone connection and we'd be happy to help"*. This was a good example of a well-directed objective communication to avoid any further confusion. Vodafone responded satisfactorily to the concerns raised by users and requested users to *DM* (direct message) their phone numbers promising that suitable action would be taken. In order to facilitate users to DM, Vodafone did *follow* them on Twitter.

IDEA *(Case Study no. 3)*

Facebook

The Facebook page of Idea[16] was highly populated by community member's posts on the wall. It could be inferred that Idea was using its Facebook page as a *listening channel*. Community members vented their complaints, raised queries on services, new schemes etc., to which Idea responded in detail. Idea welcomed criticisms and promised users that their troubles will be addressed. Whenever Idea made a post, it was either explaining users with some announcement or it was a provocative post, which would motivate users to answer the question raised. Idea also conducted polls at regular intervals of time, to engage with the users. Idea integrated its other social media channels (YouTube and Twitter) on Facebook page. Idea also uploaded videos in the videos section of its Facebook page. Idea had created an application for a major online reality contest it was organizing on *Language Barrier*[17].

Twitter

Idea did not have a bio mentioned in its Twitter handle, @ideacellular[18]. Also, it didn't have a reference to its home website. Idea used Twitter to handle customer grievances. It was interesting to observe that in addition to Facebook, it used Twitter also for the same objective. Many a time users tagged Idea for providing satisfactory service, to which Idea quickly responded and thanked them. This indicated a good gesture and mannerism by Idea.

YouTube

Idea created its YouTube channel, *IdeaCellularLtd* on May 13, 2008[19]. The broad themes of videos uploaded on this channel were

- Videos by users regarding their experience with the Idea service
- Idea TV commercials,
- Snippets of live events sponsored by Idea.

As of when this chapter was written, Idea had uploaded 100 videos, the channel had 540 subscribers, and total views of uploaded videos were 832,904[20]. Idea TV commercials had a distinct positioning as compared to commercials of other players in the industry. They hardly focused on the functional value like network coverage, tariff plans, value added services etc. It seemed they leveraged these commercials further by creating a YouTube channel.

Insights & Observations:

- Innovativeness in the style of conveying the message can keep the audience coming back and responding to the posts.
- Aggressive and outright promotion of some product may alienate the audience and thus breaking monotony of style and shifting gears to a different format (like asking audience's predictions) is important.

- In India cricket and movies are the most sought after for branding even in the traditional media. Their coming together can work wonders like the IPL cricket tournament. In the case of Airtel it can be seen that they most often tried to connect its products with these two while promoting their DTH, broadband etc.
- Contests asking for community member's inputs help creative juices flow and moreover they take it as a challenge posed by the brand. These usually see good participation as the winner gets recognition and prizes in some cases.
- The CXO interviews posted on the YouTube channel or Twitter handle or Facebook page can reflect the credibility of the brand and it also informs customers about the strategies of the firm.
- When you have a presence on multiple social media channels, try not to repeat the message across them, else it may make the experience boring for a user who is following the brand on all channels.
- Do not make direct promotional posts; try to convey the promotional message in a subtle manner by linking with any offline instance.
- Open ended contests attract more response than closed ended contests
- When you are using a social media channel for promotion, the community manager needs to come up with innovative posts that do not look repetitive in nature and at the same time should have the potential to attract as high engagement as possible.
- Instead of you doing the talking all time it would be advisable to have your customers talk on their behalf. This could be done by inviting videos from users by sharing their experience with the brand.
- If you are having multiple accounts on a same social media channel (for instance multiple Twitter handles, or multiple Facebook pages) it would be advisable to make it clear on your home website, the purpose behind each of them. This would help customers to reach the right destination and it also simplifies the community manager's job, as no repeated

clarifications need to be made.

- Try to experiment with all the features of a social media channel and think how innovatively you could make use of it. In Vodafone case study, an innovative usage of Discussions, Notes feature of the Facebook page can be noticed.
- If the link on the Facebook page wall directs to the website of a particular brand, it may result in impulse buying and also the user getting exposed to more related offerings.

10 B. Book Retailing (Dated: 20th December, 2010)

Parameters	*Flipkart*	*Dialabook*
Social media widgets provided on homepage	Yes	Partially
Social media presence	Facebook Twitter Blog	Facebook Twitter Blog
Facebook		
Welcome Fan tab	Yes	No
Info tab details	Yes	Yes
Integration with other social media tools	No	No
Community members can make post/ upload photos, videos	Yes	Yes
Applications	'Reviews'	'Polls'
Twitter		
Company name	Yes	Yes
Background image relevant to product	Yes	Yes
Location	'BLR, DEL, BOM, CCU, India'	'All across India'
Web address	Home website	Facebook page
Informative bio	No	Yes
Blog		
About blog	No	No
Blog post categories	Yes	No
Archives	Yes	No
Search facility	Yes	No

Book product category has lot of sub categories like text books, comics, fiction, non-fiction, novels, story books, self-help books, competition oriented books, etc. In India, there exists a vast unorganized retail environment which has been the major source for purchasing books. Books belonging to various categories are sold at various venues like retail shops, railway stations, bus stations, footpaths, etc. Crossword was one of the pioneers in this industry which introduced the concept of book retailing (in offline world) to the book lovers. It exposed the customers to a significant change in the way books could be bought. With the Internet penetration, many players jumped into the bandwagon offering online book retailing services. The customer behavior of purchasing books majorly is driven by the reputation of author, publisher, attractiveness of topic and price. The major value proposition that offline retailers offered was monetary discounts. However, the online retailers came up with various value propositions like book summary, book reviews, hassle free book browsing and purchasing, quicker delivery etc. This is one category where a customer's reading preference might evolve over a period of his/her lifetime and thereby increasing the chances of repurchase from the retailer, if the services offered by the retailer are satisfactory. Also, many a times books are purchased on an impulse basis. Hence, it sounds necessary for retailers to build long term relationships with customers and also keep them updated about new books (that suits their liking) that arrive in the market. Here, case studies of two online book retailers who have managed to establish their presence in customer's mind with their social media activities/initiatives is discussed.

FLIPKART *(Case Study no. 4)*

Flipkart the online book retailing firm was established in 2007 and is based at Bangalore. Initially Flipkart was involved in selling only books, however recently (as of 2010) they also started selling mobile phones, games, music and movies through their website[1].

Facebook

The Flipkart Facebook page[2] had quite a comforting message for the first time visitors – "We like you too!" For the better connect with the social media channel the like button instead of the word "like" in their message has been used. Flipkart, did not have as much any pictorial logo for its company other than the firm name which itself served as the logo. However, for the Facebook page a very insightful profile photo had been created, which had a collage of pictures of books, mobile phones, gaming remote and movies. This clearly conveyed the message about the linkage of their product offerings.

The manner in which wall posts were made was pretty refreshing. Almost every post had an image of the product being promoted (either of the cover page of the book or the mobile handset) and often when the photo was clicked it directed to the webpage where the information about that product was available on their website. This strategy could help Flipkart in two key aspects

- It increases the traffic to its website (through the weblink) and
- The picture of the product conveys an in-depth message about it. The picture also makes a post look attractive rather than a simple text message.

Once in a while a stimulating post was spotted, which called for increased engagement with the community members. For example, there were posts regarding any of the current affairs, some posts made community members to guess the title of the book etc. This was well connected to the product category, and more importantly it fuelled lot of imagination and hence the motivation for community members to comment on those posts. Each post on its wall had hundreds of "*like*" and a descent number of comments. However, extensive interaction happening between the brand and the community members could not be noticed. Though, the wall was open for any community member to post a message, we could rarely find community manager responding to them. Even any inquiry placed or a feedback on the Facebook page did not elicit a response.

Whenever a new blog post was added to its blog, it was promoted on the Facebook page and a link provided to that blog post. Many a times the post had information on the price of the product or the special offer which was available for the product at that instant. This would have signalled the customer, whether it was affordable enough and whether he/she had to make an effort to visit the website and read through the details of the product. The Facebook page also had a special "Reviews"[3] application wherein customers could express their feedback and leave a testimonial about the service provided by Flipkart. Here, a five star rating scale was used, wherein customer could rate the service apart from typing in the message. This tab created a 'special space' for customers to share their experience about the service. It was observed that on an average, just one post per day was made as against the popular belief that one needs to post often to increase the engagement with the community members. It could be inferred that the strategy adopted by Flipkart was to bank on the quality of posts rather than the frequency.

Twitter

It was noticed that Fipkart used its Twitter handle @flipkart[4] as a listening tool. Flipkart hardly made any tweet on its own, but posted hundreds of replies to the tweeters who tagged Flipkart in their tweets. It could be observed that Flipkart acknowledged almost all who had tagged it or tweeted regarding it and ensured that a reply was posted. 2,500 people *followed* Flipkart Twitter handle , while Flipkart *followed* only 13 people[5].

Blog

The Flipkart blog[6] was organized and uncluttered. The right hand panel had information on the blog post categories, search space, recent posts, recent comments, archives, and a calendar. The major themes on which the blog posts were made are interviews with authors, book reviews, list of top 10 books/movies on certain key topics, an insight on the book industry, game reviews, etc. It was observed that the informative content which would be relevant and could attract the attention for a book enthusiast. Those who purchase a book often would like to have brief information on the focus and reviews of the book, which could be satisfied by the book review posts on the blog. Some book lovers go a step ahead and would have to get as much information as possible about the author of the book. For such enthusiasts, some of the authors were interviewed and it was presented in the blog post form by Flipkart. This was a distinct rich value proposition as it met the need of a greater involvement in the book buying process.

DIAL-A-BOOK *(Case Study no. 5)*

Dial-a-book[7] was founded in 2009 and based at Delhi. It came up with an innovative customer service interface, wherein customers needed to just call or send a SMS to a mobile number (09650-457-457) to order their books.

Facebook

Dial-a-book posts on its Facebook page[8] were at a higher frequency. Dial-a-book made multiple posts in a day, and used photos of the book cover page along with its posts. However, some of its posts carried price information and some didn't. This lack of consistency which may have been done for a strategic reason was distinctly observable. A large number of community members, posted their inquiry on Dial-a-book page, to which Dial-a-book community managers replied as early as possible. Apart from the posts on book titles, Dial-a-book initiated discussions on reading habits. For example, what time of day people read most, what type of books people read during weekends, what criteria people look for before buying the books, etc. These kinds of posts, which reflected that a community member's life received attention, were observed to get a warm response. Also, Dial-a-book posted videos related to famous authors from YouTube on the page. It was noted that as community members posted their queries on the page, not only Dial-a-book responded to them, but also other fellow community members responded to it resulting in a multi-directional interaction. The reference to their website could not be located on any of their posts.

Twitter

The Twitter handle of Dial-a-book was @dialabook[9]. The first thing which can be clearly observed is the fact that Dial-a-book was *following* more number of people, than the number of people who were *following* Dial-a-book. At the time of this book, Dial-a-book *followed* 885 people, while 557 *followed* Dial-a-book[10]. Twitter was used as both the interaction channel and product promotion channel. Dial-a-book regularly tweeted about various books, with almost complete information including the price. Dial-a-book made it a point to acknowledge the positive feedback, which is very essential to pamper the community members.

Blog

The blog as it was observed had not attained a high level of maturity. The blog posts were on varied themes like interview with author, company information, press coverage etc. The blog could have been made more informative for engaging with the customers.

***Insights & Observations*:**

- Each social networking channel could be used primarily for a specific purpose. Flipkart primarily used Facebook page for promoting its products, while Twitter was used mainly to listen what customers were talking about them and to interact with the customers.
- The content posted either on Facebook or Twitter should have match and appear relevant with the product category and the product that the firm is selling. This has a higher chance of grabbing the interest of prospective customers and sustaining the patronage of existing ones.
- The integration between the social media channels should be leveraged for better distribution of content and increased engagement with the community members.
- More stress should always be laid on quality as compared to frequency of posts. Even if one post is not perceived well by the target audience, it can cause huge damage.
- Blogs could be an ideal information repository, which may be cross-posted on social networks to increase the web traffic and can serve as a "food for thought "processing agents amongst community members to fuel interaction.
- Blog posts should be on relevant topics, which should add value that readers seek. This may be in the form of more knowledge about a particular subject or person related to the purchase. This helps build a positive image and ultimately increases the chances of sale.
- The community manager should further show a more caring attitude that brand has towards the members. Continued acknowledgement and recognition of the community members is one such way.
- The posts perceived as "Informative" or having an "Infotainment" quotient for the community members would fuel higher interaction and hence increased engagement with the brand.

10 C. Accessories (Dated: 26th December, 2010)

Parameters	*Fastrack*	*Wildcraft*
Social media widgets provided on homepage	Partly	Yes
Social media presence	Facebook Twitter YouTube	Facebook Twitter YouTube Blog
Facebook		
Welcome Fan tab	No	Yes
Info tab details	Yes	Yes
Integration with other social media tools	No	Yes
Community members can make post/upload photos, videos	Yes	Yes
Applications	'Hip Hop' 'Store Locator' 'FT Girl' 'Kickass Cards'	'Buy Now' 'Chat'
Twitter		
Company name	Yes	Yes
Background image relevant to product	Yes	Yes
Location	No	Bangalore
Web address	Home website	Home website
Informative bio	Yes	No
YouTube		
About company	No	Yes
Video themes	• TV Commercials	• TV Commercials • Promotional videos
Blog		
About blog	—	No
Blog post categories	—	Yes
Archives	—	Yes
Search facility	—	Yes

Prima facie, accessories was initially associated mainly with women.However nowadays we observe a lot of accessories related to males have found their place in the market. A wide variety of accessories based on sports, movies, etc. are available. Also, there now exist accessories for specific purposes like sports event, party, wedding, tour, trekking etc. With the large number of youngsters in India, this category is likely to make further inroads in the customer's life. Here we discuss the social media efforts made by two brands Fastrack and Wildcraft to engage their customers.

FASTRACK *(Case Study no. 6)*

In this era where patience levels have gone down considerably, the very name identifies 'youthful' aspirations of a 'Fast Track'. The level of awareness of Fastrack is considered to be high amongst youth. Fastrack was initially launched as a sub-brand of Titan, and later on in 2005 it was spun off as an independent brand of watches[1]. As time passed Fastrack added new products to its assortment and as of now is known for products like bags, belts, wallets, wrist bands etc. which are targeted at youth. Fastrack has positioned its product as one those provide *cool* quotient to the youngsters.

Facebook

The first attractive aspect of the Facebook page[2] was the profile photo. When this case study was written, the Facebook page had used 32 profile photos[3]. In general, brands would always like themselves to be associated with a particular logo so that it registers with and is then identified by the customers. However, it's interesting to note that Fastrack was applying the opposite strategy and it kept on changing the profile picture of its Facebook page, probably giving more freshness to the look of the page, so that community members don't get bored seeing the same image often. Just below the profile picture, Fastrack had provided other touch points like how to reach Fastrack on mobile and Twitter. The major attraction of content strategy followed by Fastrack was contests. They ran variety of contests on various themes such as - "Hip Hop"[4], "Scan My Bag", "Denim Collection"etc. One million Facebook fans celebration, offered 10 lucky fans from Mumbai and Pune tickets for *NH7 Weekender festival* at Pune etc. The contests created did not involve just answering to a few questions, but they required a substantial deeper involvement from the community members. The community members were required to visit the link to the contest on the website and play some game, solve a puzzle, express their thoughts and then the best entries were judged to be winners. In addition to such major contests, Fastrack also had some impromptu contests wherein fans were required to answer the question in next 30 minutes, contests based on upcoming movies etc. As the target audience of the brand was youngsters, the contest based approach to engage with community members were a great move as they fuelled excitement and challenge to the members on a regular basis. Apart from contests, Fastrack also used the Facebook page to announce about new stores that were set up, shared Fastrack commercials, product assortment pictures to get the conversation going with community members.

The "Hip Hop" application had been linked to the website, where community members could play games and enter the contest. The "Store Locator"[5] application on Facebook page should be very helpful to the community members. The application provided detailed address of store in a particular city. The application also had a Google map embedded in it, which helped users quickly identify the location of the store on the map. This application was extremely user friendly and very valuable to users. The "FT Girl"[6] application focused on the female customers. It included wallpapers, screensavers and a small poll related to women. This application seemed to have been included to ensure that Fastrack had an equal appeal to customers of both genders. The "Kickass cards"[7] application appeared to be adding *cool* quotient to the Facebook page and had an excellent connect with the target audience.

The choice of applications by Fastrack was both informative in nature and helped to maintain enthusiasm, *cool* quotient amongst the community members.

Twitter

The Twitter handle of Fastract was @fastrack[8]. The background of the Twitter handle displayed a scene from their latest commercial featuring cricketer, Virat Kohli and also had an image of watch, which was the key offering of the Fastrack. The display of home website address and their Facebook page on the background was attractive.

The Twitter bio had just one sentence, *"India's most loved youth fashion brand!"*. An unique theme or purpose for which Fastrack was intending to utilize it's presence on Twitter was not identifiable. With a closer look, it could be deciphered that Fastrack used this channel for multiple purposes which included promoting their contests, congratulating winners of contests etc. They also *retweeted* tweets from their brand ambassadors like Genelia D'souza, Virat Kohli. This could have been for grabbing the attention of the youth adding a variety to the tweets rather than monotonously engaging them with Fastrack communication

YouTube

Fastrack created its YouTube channel on November 14, 2007[9]. Fastrack used this channel majorly to promote the commercials. As and when Fastrack came up with a new TV commercial, it was uploaded on this channel. When this case study was written, Fastrack had uploaded just 30 videos (for the last three years), the channel had 103 subscribers, and total views of uploaded videos were 179,245[10]. As compared to its Facebok and Twitter presence, this channel was not utilized as much. The comments made by subscribers were left unattended and thus showed lack of 'engaging'.

WILDCRAFT *(Case Study no. 7)*

Wildcraft provides good quality gears for adventurous outings. They also provide corporate gear, campus gear, outdoor gear, travel gear, active wear and MTV gear. As of December 2010, they had 15 stores in 3 cities[11].

Facebook

Similar to Fastrack, Wildcraft too had an impressive profile photo. Right below the profile photo, Wildcraft had enlisted all the contact points for community members like website, Twitter handle, phone number, email for any queries. As done by Wildcraft, providing phone number and email for further queries may reduce the chances of community members posting their queries on the wall. This would lead to the wall getting less cluttered as the posts regarding complains could be lesser. The Facebook page had an impressive Welcome tab, where in the adventurous feeling is triggered with a message,

"The Outdoors lie within"[12]. The following were the major themes on which posts were made on the Facebook page - product promotions, sharing of blog post, contests, posts that asked community members to visit Wildcraft's Twitter handle and follow the interaction between customers and founder Dinesh, media coverage of Wildcraft. The majority of the posts were on product promotions and the sharing of blog posts. Community members too shared their adventurous trip experience with the photo, because of which it was noticed that there were 581 photos uploaded by community members (as and when this case study was written). This provided a place for community members to share their experience, reflected the commitment that community members had towards the Facebook page and also might have smoothened the content generation process of the Wildcraft to some extent. As community members shared their experience with photos, it invited lot of engagement amongst the community members. For example, there were instances when fellow community members inquired about place on seeing its photo and got further details about the place. Wildcraft made a sincere effort to take feedback from community members on products through surveys. They floated a survey and community members were requested to fill it. They also had an instant chat application on the Facebook page.

Twitter

The Twitter handle of Wildcraft was @wildcraftnews[13]. The positioning of the Twitter handle was distinct and effectively communicated. On reaching the handle, the first thing one would notice was the clear message on the background which reads, *"ASK DINI A channel for getting answers to all your OUTDOORS & ADVENTURE queries. Just prefix your query with @wildcraftnews"*. Now having read this instruction, it becomes easy to figure out the purpose of having this handle –it's for handling queries from the community members. Any query related to visiting adventurous places for trekking, sports etc. was entertained here. Also, this channel was used to share tips on various adventurous activities like which dress was adept for a particular place, list of medical items to be kept during the journey, kind of bags to be carried for trekking, instructions for tying the belt should be tied etc. Wildcraft made careful use of *hashtags* such as #rafting, #scuba #diving, #trekking, #hiking, #bungee #jumping, #snorkeling etc. This wide usage of relevant *hashtags* would have increased the chances of Wildcraft channel appearing in the Twitter search results, which might result in more followers and probably more business. As and when this case study was written about 557 tweeters *followed* Wildcraft, while Wildcraft *followed* 462 tweeters[14].

YouTube

Wildcraft created its YouTube channel on October 07, 2009. The broad themes of videos uploaded on this channel were – a) commercials, c) promotional videos. As when this chapter was written, Wildcraft had uploaded just 6 videos, the channel had 5 subscribers, and total views of uploaded videos were 2,165. Wildcraft seemed to be using this channel on a regular basis, as it was noticed that only 6 videos were uploaded over a period of one year.

Blog

The major focus of the blog was to inform customers about various adventurous destinations in the country. The blog posts on destinations were very informative describing the climate, key site seeing places which could be explored, important do's and don'ts etc. which a visitor would require. To generate such kind of informative blog posts, adequate research needs to be done and the efforts put in by Wildcraft team appeared extensive. At the end of each blog post an indirect promotion was made about any of the product offering, which is an innovative blogging strategy.

Insights & Observations

- Contests fuel excitement and thrill amongst the community members. However, contests need to have adequate level of involvement from the community members.
- A mix of both informative and hedonic (playful) applications would be helpful for brands that wish to position their *cool* quotient.
- Relevant usage of *hashtags* increase the chances of appearing in the Twitter search results, hence they should be used judiciously.

- Blog posts apart from product offerings could focus on end user benefits, which would be a great value addition for the community members and will keep them engaged thus sustaining traffic.
- A detailed bio on the different offerings (products) can be helpful for customers who are not aware of the company.

10 D. Automobiles (Dated: 30th December, 2010)

Parameters	*Mahindra Scorpio*	*Tata Nano*	*Maruti Suzuki SX4*
Social media widgets provided on homepage	Yes	No	Yes
Social media presence	Facebook Twitter YouTube Flickr Orkut	Facebook Twitter	Facebook Twitter YouTube Orkut
Facebook			
Welcome Fan tab	Yes	No	Yes
Info tab details	Yes	Yes	Yes
Integration with other social media tools	No	No	Yes
Community members can make post/ upload photos, videos	Yes	Yes	Yes
Applications	'What's New'	No	'Chat with us'
Twitter			
Company name	Yes	Yes	Yes
Background image relevant to product	Yes	No	Yes
Location	India	All over India	India
Web address	Home website	Home website	Facebook Facebook page
Informative bio	Yes	No	Yes
YouTube			
About company		Yes	No
Video themes		TV commercials	TV commercials

In this section four-wheeler automobiles product category is discussed. It has always been a dream of most of the Indians to own a car at least once in a lifetime. Bank loans have fuelled the market expansion of this category, as it has facilitated the purchase to a great extent. The increasing income levels have also substantially triggered the car ownership amongst the youngsters. Cars are now available in India for almost every customer segment, right from first time buyers to luxury car owners. Cars are purchased occasionally, in some cases for a lifetime, and hence the way and level of engagement of the brands with their customers needs to be extremely well thought. The case studies discussed would help readers, visualize the engagement strategy followed by the brands.

MAHINDRA SCORPIO *(Case Study no. 8)*

Facebook

The Facebook page[1] had an impressive video in the welcome tab. The profile picture highlighted the achievement of the community as a whole, as it indicated that community size had reached 3,00,000 fans. The tab *What's New* was meant largely for entertainment purpose. It had applications such as *"How Mighty Muscular Are You?"* and *"Great Escape"*[2]. These applications were pretty engaging and use of such applications had the potential to increase the chances of engagement with the community members. It also had a poll and contest for fans to upload their Scorpio photos on the community. The Facebook page was integrated to its Twitter and YouTube channels. Photos were the major content strategy of engagement for this Facebook page. A large number of photos were uploaded by the brand and about 3,500 photos[3] were uploaded by the community members about their cars. It was evident from the photos that community members were eager to impress each other and intended to flaunt their prized possession. On a daily basis, many community members uploaded photos of their cars which were liked and appreciated by fellow community members. The contest was run for the best Scorpio photos uploaded by the community members and every week a winner was selected. During the launch of Mahindra Thar, the Facebook page was used for its promotion and videos uploaded on YouTube channel were shared here. The participation from the brand on the community was very sparse. The posts made by brand had substantial time period interval between them. However, the community members regularly discussed about buying the new car, some issues they faced with the existing car, trips they made with their car etc, which were equally responded by the fellow community members. The Facebook page has been an ideal channel for the community members to share their experience with the product.

Twitter

The Twitter handle of Mahindra Scorpio was @MahindraScorpio[4]. The Twitter background of Mahindra Scorpio is attractive with pictures of the car and the slogan, *"Mighty Muscular Scorpio – Nothing else will do"*. The bio includes description of the car features – *smokes less, drinks less with micro hybrid technology.* The bio was able to describe the product, however a user may not understand the purpose of the Twitter handle, and how he/she can use this to communicate with the brand. The website address provided is that of Scorpio's Facebook page and not the home website, which indicates the confidence the brand has on the content and engagement strategy maintained at its Facebook page. Though about 1400 people were *following*, the brand hardly *followed* 8 people[5] (figures as and when this case study was written). This indicated two aspects –

- All communications happened open and users were not required to use Direct Message (DM) feature,
- Brand was not interested in the daily lives of the followers.

Mahindra ran contests on its Facebook page. The winners of these contests were informed and congratulated here too. They also handled customer grievances regarding servicing of vehicle. They humbly apologized for the errors committed by dealers and asked the customer to provide the details of the dealer on email at customercare@mahindra.com or inform them on designated telephone numbers. In order to maintain the enthusiasm of the community members, Mahindra also shared some pictures of Scorpio cars in adventurous locations. Hence, Mahindra used this channel not just as a grievance addressable medium, but also ensured that its followers remained excited about the product. It seemed that though the major purpose of the channel was to handle customer grievances, the community members were entertained with some additional content.

YouTube

Mahindra Scorpio created its YouTube channel on March 13, 2009[6]. Mahindra Scorpio used this channel majorly to promote their commercials and their sponsored events. As and when Mahindra Scorpio came up with a new TV commercial, they uploaded that commercial on this channel. As and when this case study was written, Mahindra Scorpio had uploaded just 20 videos, the channel had 48 subscribers, and total views of uploaded videos were 71, 486[7]. The adventure positioning of the brand is maintained in all videos. Surprisingly, any interaction could not be noticed happening over this channel. There was just one comment made.

Flickr

Mahindra created its presence on Flickr in August, 2009[8]. The photographs shared were of following themes – photos shared by proud Scorpio owners as part of their Travelogue experience, photos uploaded by customers as part of various contests that were run by Scorpio, launch of new model (Mahindra Scorpio Xtreme), photos of exhibition displays where Scorpio participated, autocar performance show photos and photos uploaded by "Further & Beyond"[2]. Mahindra had uploaded around 200 photos[9] on this channel but any interaction happening on the channel could not be noticed.

MARUTI SX4 *(Case Study no. 9)*

Facebook

The profile image of the Facebook page[10] highlighted the contest *Bite My Dust*, wherein community members were asked to design a T-shirt which expressed their excitement about four-wheel drive. The Facebook page had been integrated with other social media channels – Twitter and YouTube. The *Bite My Dust*[11] application had information about the contest and had access to designs that were so far uploaded by the contestants. The *SX4 Green*[12] application had a bright picture of the new CNG model and a link to brochure was provided just below the picture. A Live Chat support was provided on the Facebook page, wherein users could key in their personal details (name, email, phone number and city) and start conversing with the customer support desk regarding the car. Maruti used photos extensively in their content strategy. The photos from auto shows where Maruti SX4 participated were uploaded (82 when this case study was written). Also community members uploaded photos (37 when this case study was written) of their SX4[13]. The photos uploaded by community members were well received by the community, as we noticed many likes and comments were made by the community members. We noticed that Maruti made posts with substantial interval between posts, however community members were very active and they posted their queries on the wall (as the wall was open for community members to make posts) and many of them wrote testimonials for the car and shared their real life experience of possessing their dream car. Even before the Maruti could respond the query, we found that fellow community members tried to answer the query and there prevailed an interaction between the community members. At some placed we noticed that the community manager instead of responding to the queries raised by community members, asked them to make use of the Live Chat Support feature.

Maruti mainly made posts on contests and shared details (along with photos, as community members could relive the moment)·about car rallies which they conducted at various places. They also made posts on specifications of the car, dealer locator feature on their website etc. which would help customers in their search and evaluation stages of their buying process. At regular intervals they also made posts about their presence on Twitter, Orkut and requested community members to follow the brand at these channels too. It was noticed that there was no convincing purpose elicited to the community members for why should a user follow the same brand on multiple social media channels. In one post Maruti thanked the customers from Gujarat who owned SX4 CNG model. The main attraction of this post[14] was that it had the message written in Gujarati language (along with the message in the English). It was an innovative 'localized messaging' strategy to build connects with the community members from the state. Both Maruti and community members tried to position the car as "*sexy*". It appeared that the purpose of this community was to position SX4 as a *macho* brand.

Twitter

The Twitter handle of Maruti SX4 was @marutisuzukisx4[15]. Similar to that of Mahindra Scorpio, Maruti too had a attractive Twitter background with picture of the car. The bio ensured users that it was an official Twitter handle and provided an email for contact (social@sx4bymaruti.com). The website address provided was that of its Facebook page and not of the home website. The Twitter handle seemed to be created recently, because as of now it had just 79 *followers* and Maruti was *following* 62 members[16]. The main purpose of this Twitter handle was not explicit. Majority of the tweets just mentioned about one or other activity that was happening on their Facebook page and the link was provided for the same. There was also an excessive use of hashtags (#auto, #motoring, #cars, #maruti, #India, #SX4).

YouTube

Maruti Suzuki SX4 created its YouTube channel on September, 4, 2009[17]. Maruti had customized its channel in an attractive manner. The four tabs – Experience, Live Chat, Style and BuySX4 directed the user to the home website. Also, Maruti had explicitly made the social media presence visible by placing the icons of those websites. They had maintained playlist in a disciplined manner which included videos on three themes – SX4 in the News, videos uploaded by user and TV commercials. Maruti had uploaded just 28 videos (for the last one year), thc channel had just 9 subscribers, and total views of uploaded videos were 5,512[18]. Any significant interaction happening over this channel could not be noticed. There were no comments on the channel.

Flickr

Maruti created its Flickr channel in September, 2010[19]. Photos of the car were uploaded and also some photos of an autoshow where some Bollywood stars got clicked with the car. Within couple of months of the channel creation, Maruti had so far uploaded about 70 photos[20] to the channel, however no interaction was observed in this channel.

TATA NANO *(Case Study no. 10)*

Facebook

The Tata Nano Facebook page[21] was mainly used to share news about the car – promotions, award won at design competition and to conduct contests for the community members. Any specific brand related posts made by the Tata Nano on the wall were hardly visible.

These posts might have created enthusiasm amongst the community members to start discussion and get into an engagement mode. Many community members posted their queries regarding the product, its availability, price, maintenance etc. which were replied by fellow community members more often than the brand. Further, it was noticed that the posts made by the community members were not acknowledged largely by the brand. Even when community members congratulated the brand for having won the award at an international design competition, the acknowledgements were missing. It's always been a best practice for a community to acknowledge it's member's activity as they acknowledge that of the brand's. This makes the communication smoother and helps understand if the post has been seen or not. It was also noticed that a particular member was participating repeatedly on many posts. It may be possible that the member happened to be an ardent fan as the member was very knowledgeable about the product. If brands had such enthusiastic members, even if they are less in numbers, such *influencers* are vital for branding and engagement. The knowledge and passion that these influencers have could be leveraged in the benefit of the brand and the community.

Twitter

The Twitter handle of Tata Nano was @tatanano_tweets[22]. The Twitter background of Tata Nano was very simple. The bio read, *"Official Tata Nano Tweets – from the makers of the Nano"*. The home website detail was provided in the website section, unlike the link to Facebook page, as it was seen in case of Mahindra Scorpio and Maruti SX4. About 630 users *followed* the handle and Tata Nano *followed* about 225 users[23]. The timeline indicated that tweets weren't made on a daily basis and there were substantial gaps between two consecutive tweets. It was observed that this channel was used for broadcasting tweets on varied themes. The themes of tweets that could be noticed were – award won by Nano at some international design competition, congratulating winners of contest, Nano news in media, promotion of book "Small Wonder" which was based on Nano story, Facebook posts reposted here, offline road shows etc. Twitter was not often used with the primary purpose of a broadcasting channel and thus it would be interesting to see if this approach would yield any interaction amongst the community members.

Insights & Observations:

- One common aspect about the Facebook page of all three brands discussed here is, it was used primarily as a channel for customers to express their feelings, experiences about the product, rather than brand initiating the talk. It is interesting to observe a similar strategy across all three brands, wherein community members took the initiative of engagement. It could not be concluded though that if this sort of engagement was a deliberate choice or it reached this stage over a period of time.
- Reflecting the positioning of brand in various channels requires strategic planning to the minutes details on content strategy.
- Significantly less interaction was seen occurring on content oriented channels like Flickr and YouTube, unlike relationship oriented channels Facebook and Twitter. A probable reason may be lesser user to user connection (like making friends etc.) in these channels which may have lead to users not getting interested to share their views. This could be because even after making an effort to comment on these photos or videos, they might not receive any reply from fellow users and hence the vicious cycle continues. An innovative manner of interaction needs to be planned to fuel discussions on these content oriented channels.
- Usage of multiple hashtags indicates the desperateness of the brand to get noticed amongst the tweeters, which might not be an appreciative move.
- The brand should provide convincing reasons to users in order to convince them to follow the brand on multiple social media channels.
- Innovative applications that resemble the positioning of the product help in increasing the engagement with community members.
- Customers are in need of an ideal channel to express their feelings about the product; however some planning needs to be done on social media channels before opening the space for customers to jump in.
- It is very essential to acknowledge each other's activity, as in virtual medium the other members would not know if you

have seen the activity, unless you make an effort to acknowledge it. This is especially needed to be practiced by the brand as it would build community member's confidence on the brand community.

- Identifying relevant influencers in the community and leveraging them for the development of the community and brand is very essential. It needs to be carefully tracked that who are participating, what are their views, whether fellow community members listen to that influencer's views, how influential he/she is in real life etc. needs to be considered.
- It is good to have a Live Chat Support .However the community managers should try to settle the query at the post itself. This will reduce the additional effort a user has to make. Also as the interaction would be visible to other community members, it can solve the purpose of answering their queries automatically. The transparent interaction on Facebook should be done to the greatest extent possible and only in special cases the community members should be asked to take the support service.

10 E. FMCG (Dated: 2nd January, 2011)

Parameters	*Ching's Secret*	*Hippo*	*Waghbakri*	*Kurkure*	*Happydent*
Social media widgets provided on homepage	Yes	Yes	Yes	Yes	Yes
Social media presence	Facebook Twitter YouTube	Facebook Twitter	Facebook Twitter	Facebook YouTube	Facebook
Facebook					
Welcome Fan tab	Yes	No	No	No	No
Info tab details	Yes	Yes	Yes	Yes	Yes
Integration with other social media tools	No	No	No	No	No
Community members can make post/ upload photos, videos	Yes	Yes	No	Yes	Yes
Applications	No	No	'Tea Lounge'	'Click-n-Win'	No

Twitter					
Company name	Yes	Yes	Yes	—	—
Background image relevant to product	Yes	Yes	Yes	—	—
Location	Mumbai, India	'Hippo say right after hunger'	India	—	—
Web address	Facebook Facebook page	Facebook Facebook page	Retail website	—	—
Informative bio	Yes	Yes	No	—	—
YouTube					
About company	Yes	—	Yes	—	—
Video themes	Recipes	—	TV commercials	—	—

Fast Moving Consumer Goods (FMCG) is the category ,as the name suggests, involves frequent purchases and at regular intervals. It includes foods, drinks, confectionaries, etc. A majority of the goods under this category is purchased at the beginning of the month, as suited to the Indian customer purchase process and repurchased towards the end of month or when the stocks last , which are termed as refills. Apart from these two planned purchase instances, there is also an impulse purchase mode FMCG products are mostly sold in this country through mom and pop stores (commonly known as *kirana* stores). The competition is intense amongst the numerous local brands, regional brands, national brands. This process becomes even more challenging due to the vast geographical spread of the country and brands have to strive extensively to maintain their availability at each and every touch point. Taking into account this scenario, building and then sustaining customer loyalty is highly challenging. Social media could be used by brands to build consistent engagement with the customers, and this section enlists social media activities/ initiatives of five brands.

CHING'S SECRET *(Case Study no. 11)*

Facebook

The brand had one of the best Welcome tabs we would have discussed in this book. The welcome had an attractive picture of some of its product offerings along with a clear message *click above and like now to enjoy exclusive recipes, contests, quizzes and video jokes*[1]. It had everything in it – eye catching display, clear action message and crystal clear objective of the Facebook page. The profile picture had the brand logo along with a picture of one of their product offering. As mentioned in the welcome tab the engagement with fans was made with the help of informative recipes, contests, quizzes etc. The brand made extensive use of pictures and videos along with their posts to bring in good aesthetic feeling for the fans. The posts were well received by the fans as they received hundreds of likes and comments. We could feel that fans enjoyed a lot by conversing with the brand. The posts matched the current affairs and the product offerings and mostly were positioned in a contest format, which ensured that fans would comment on it.

Twitter

The Twitter handle of Ching's Secret was @Chingssecret[2]. The Twitter background was very interesting and matched the offerings made by Ching. Their slogan *Ching's Khao Baki Bhool Jao* however got hid behind the Twitter logo. The bio was very detailed and also had its website and Wikipedia link mentioned in it. The bio details about the products offered by the brand, but don't reveal its purpose of being on Twitter or how should community members use this route to converse with the brand. The website reference was given to its Facebook page. We have seen this tactic followed by brands in earlier case studies too, when brands provide the website details of their Facebook page rather than the home website, which provides a direct signal to the brands that brand is willing to engage with the customers and not just there to sell their products. As and when this case study was written around 500 community members followed the brand, while the brand followed around 1800 members[3]. The strategy could be to follow as many people as possible, in the anticipation that they start following the brand in return. Customers shared their experience of consuming the products on Twitter. Ching's Secret acknowledged this behavior, appreciated some suggestions provided by the community members, helped community members is using the right product by guiding them about the offerings etc. Ching's Secret also engaged in conversations about the social media marketing phenomenon with some social media agency founders, which might be irrelevant for those who are following the brand. Also the brand had some conversations with individuals which were far apart from the purpose of the product offering. The unrelated discussions clutter the timeline of followers, which might have a negative impact in the future.

YouTube

Ching's Secret created its YouTube channel on May 15, 2009[4]. Ching's Secret used this channel majorly to promote their products in a subtle manner by uploading videos on various Chinese recipes. The videos hosted by a hostess showed a chef preparing variety of Chinese dishes. We found that in the initial period of this channel, Ching's Secret had uploaded couple of videos of their TV commercials, however they discontinued doing that and later on had all videos on Chinese recipes. This tactic absolutely connected with the product offering and would help in retaining brand name in the customer's mind. The average length of the video was around 4 minutes, which is exceptional considering the trickiness to demonstrate a complicated concept of recipes. As when this case study was written, Ching's Secret had uploaded just 107 videos, the channel had 814 subscribers (a phenomenal figure considering other case studies discussed in this book), and total views of uploaded videos were 7,33, 586[5] (which again is an outstanding figure). Every video had an embedded message *Visit Ching's Secret on Facebook* and the link was provided. They have done well to direct the traffic from YouTube and Twitter to Facebook page. Also, they provided the url of home website and Twitter handle. Another interesting aspect was that below every video, the details of ingredients and preparation method was provided. The complete information about the recipe even in the text format is very appreciable. This channel had it all, informative text, video and a great connect with the offering.

HIPPO *(Case Study no. 12)*

Facebook

Here was the most surprising information. The brand was rarely active on its Facebook page[6]. The Facebook page was created in November, 2009 and since then just 10 posts were made by the brand till November, 2010. The last post made by the brand was in November, 2010. We have normally seen brands leveraging their Facebook page better than any of their other social media presence, but here lies the counter-intuitive example. However, the fans of the Facebook page made some posts, to which the brand didn't respond. The purpose behind creating a presence on Facebook page and not engaging with community members on the channel could not be deciphered. This kind of activity might create some dissonance amongst the users who would reach the Facebook page and see no real engagement happening there. The Info tab had website reference of Twitter handle and the brand's home website.

Twitter

The Twitter handle of Hippo was @HelloMeHippo[7]. The Twitter background of the Hippo handle represented the logo of the brand (the Hippo face). The brand had an impressive bio, which not only introduced user to its offerings but also details their message - *Hippo make munchies to fight hunger. Because world be better if no one hungry. Hippo say anything that not kill Hippo'll only make Hippo better hunger-fighter*[8]. The website link was directed to the brand's home website which had various features like polls, games, idea sharing feature (where users could share their ideas on ways to eradication of hunger) etc. It is appreciative to have a home website with engagement features, which sends a clear message to the customer that irrespective of the channel, brand is eager to converse with them. The location had an interesting description – *Hippo say right after hunger.* As and when this case study was written around 1400 followers followed the brand and the brand in return followed around 325 followers[9]. The language used for tweeting was very impressive, it didn't seem as if it was a deliberate conversation, but it was very informal and the brand tried to exhibit the personality of the brand through the Hippo image. Every tweet started with words like *Hippo say, Hippo think, Hippo ask* etc. which was very interesting. Such a way of addressing followers is appreciative as it builds humour and ensures better connect with the followers, instead of a very formal language. The brand had a message that because of hunger, anti-social activities prevail in the society, and hence they are there to eradicate hunger from the society and free society from the anti-social activities. The conversations that happened through tweets always emphasized the cause for which the brand stood and motivated followers to consume the product in a very subtle manner. This was a very interesting way to convince customers to consume the product instead of traditional methods of positioning the food product based on its ingredients or health perspective. The brands also motivated people to join the cause for which the brand stood, by having nutritious food and at right time. The followers when informed brand about the unavailability of the brand at some nearby shop, the brand took details from the follower and ensured them that the stock would be replenished soon at that store. Majority of tweets were replies to the followers, which clearly indicated that brand had succeeded to a great extent by maintaining conversation with the followers. The interesting aspect of the tweets was that tweets didn't have any links to their Facebook page, which indicated that Hippo treated Twitter handle as an independent channel and tried to complete the conversation on this channel itself rather than redirecting to other channels. This exhibits the confidence the brand has on its Twitter presence. This is a great learning for us, on how a particular social network could be used independent of other social networks. It is very easy to cross-post messages from other social networks (which many brands follow) however it needs great planning and patience to sustain interaction on a particular channel independent of others.

WAGHBAKRI *(Case Study no. 13)*

Facebook

The profile picture on Waghbakri's Facebook page[10] was very attractive and picture of a model sipping tea from a cup, which had the company's name on it. The logo of the company was made visible at the left handside panel of the timeline. A message, *"Different People, Different Tastes, Different Teas, One Tea Group"* was used, which clearly portrayed the message that the brand offered wide variety of products that would match the needs of varied customers. The Info tab had detailed description of the company overview, products and website section. The brand was very active on Facebook page. The posts were made using some eye-catching pictures. The message on posts revolved mostly around the product. It was surprising to see that brand also made posts that had movie reviews and movie trailers (No One Killed Jessica, Dhobi Ghat, Guzaarish, Crook: It's Good to be Bad). The brand made posts that had close relation with the current events, festivals, brand's media coverage etc. We noticed that posts were well received by the fans and the brand received descent no. of likes and comments. It was encouraging to see that brand maintained conversation with fans through comments. The conversations seemed to be reflecting the fact that brand wanted itself to be part of everyone's life at any particular stage. The Facebook page had a special tab *Tea Lounge*, where details regarding the retail tea shop opened at Mumbai are shared. The detailed description of the lounge was provided and the brand invited fans to visit the lounge and feel the experience. Overall we felt that brand had been successful in maintaining conversation with the brand on various topics, however we are unsure how much did such diverse conversation help the brand.

Twitter

The Twitter background of the Waghbakri handle @waghbakri[11] had the same features as the profile picture of the Facebook page. Just the background here was customized to a yellow colour. The bio section just had one sentence, *Waghbakri Tea Group*. The website link routed to the online retailing website named as www.buytea.com, where customers could buy the tea online. This was an interesting strategy, wherein the users would be directed to the e-commerce site rather than the customer engagement destination (Facebook page) or the home website. As that of Ching's Secret no. of users whom the brand followed was almost four times that of the no. of followers of the brand (580 vs. 130, as and when this case study was written[12]). It was surprising to see that many tweets just had an url, and no message. This would not be an appreciative manner of tweeting, as users might not click on the url without knowing what message they would face. Moreover, the tweets didn't seem to be erupting any conversation with the followers. The tweets (urls) mainly redirected the user to their Facebook page post. It seemed as if the brand didn't want to converse with users on Twitter and somehow wanted users to visit the Facebook page and converse there. A few of the links directed to the YouTube videos, which seemed to be having no relation with the brand.

KURKURE *(Case Study no. 14)*

Facebook

The profile picture of the Facebook page[13] had its logo, which was well placed. The Info tab had detailed description of the company and the products offered. The Facebook page had a special tab *Click-n-Win,* which was a contest, wherein fans were required to upload the fun-filled picture of their family and the pictures that received maximum number of likes were supposed to be given away prizes. The contest did have association with the brand positioning. As and when this case study was written, about 178 pictures[14] were uploaded by the fans, majorly due to the contest that was floated by the brand. The contest was well received by the fans, as we noticed that most of the posts on the wall were made by the fans as they uploaded their picture for the contest. Apart from the contest picture, fans made posts sharing their liking for the brand, to which the brand responded immediately by thanking them. The brand rarely made wall posts. We noticed that couple of fans (which seemed to be bots) made comment (along with a url) on posts, which asked other fans to *like* the page. Such, comments could have been moderated by the community manager; however we found them to be left as it is. The contest seemed to be the driving factor of engagement for the Facebook page. It would be interesting to observe how this strategy would have assisted the brand's social media objective.

YouTube

Kurkure created its YouTube channel on May 31, 2006[15]. Though the channel was created way back in 2006, we noticed that videos were added just in December, 2010. Kurkure used this channel majorly to promote their products by uploading videos of their TV commercials and some customer experience videos. The customers who had participated in some contest and had won, were video shooted and they shared with experience with the product. As and when this case study was written, Kurkure had uploaded just 12 videos, and total views of uploaded videos were mere 305[16]. Unfortunately, the channel wasn't subscribed by any user.

HAPPYDENT *(Case Study no. 15)*

Facebook

The profile picture itself gave an upfront message about the Facebook page[17]. The Info tab had the description of the contest in the company overview section and no detail about the product was mentioned. The picture had the message of *Sparkling Smiles Contest,* which was the fundamental basis of engagement for this Facebook page. The brand encouraged fans to upload pictures of theirs and their friends with smiling faces, and those that received maximum comments were judged to be winners and each person in the picture received a mug with their group picture printed on it as the prize. The concept of the contest matched well with the product and we noticed that about 14,900 pictures[18] (as and when this case study was written) were uploaded by the fans, which shows that fans have well-received the message. As and when the fans uploaded their pictures, the brand then collated some of them (usually 4 to 6 of them were selected) and announced the contest amongst those pictures.

After a specified time, the picture that received maximum number of comments was announced as winner. The Facebook page had uploaded its TV commercials in the video tab. A poll was run to know the customer liking towards their TV commercials. This Facebook page is a great example wherein the brand has provided the platform for fans to exhibit their talent and converse with each other. The brand just had the moderation role and as the content was produced by the fans themselves, the repeated efforts for the moderators were minimal (except the task of selecting relevant pictures for the contest). It would be interesting to see how long would the brand be successful in sustaining community member's interest and attention on the Facebook page with just one single engagement tactic.

Insights & Observations:

- Following 3 or 4 times the users, than the number following the brand might reflect the desperate need of the brand to gain followers. This might happen if the brand is unclear of the channel objectives or lacks relevant content to engage with the users.
- The community manager should not try to build personal relationships using the brand's channel. If this happens there are many conversations which happen between individuals but they are totally irrelevant to the brand followers.
- Every url tweeted through Twitter should have a message that gives description of the content that the user would face on clicking the url. Not having any message might substantially reduce the interest level of the user to click on it, and hence might go unnoticed.
- For some product categories informal language (or tone) used in the posts/tweets might bring an informal feeling, which might fuel better connection with the followers. The followers won't feel as if they are engaging with the brand for some purpose, but they would feel as if they are engaging with their friend, which has a very positive sign of building relationships.
- If the brand has a presence on multiple social networks, it doesn't necessarily imply one should cross-post message from one network to the other, just with the thought of driving

traffic. It could be beneficial to maintain one network presence for a particular objective and build conversation with that objective in mind.

- If you are not sure of how to use a particular social media channel, it would be risky to create the presence and not participate in it. It is better to delete the presence and concentrate only where the brand is comfortable of engaging with the customers.
- It's advisable to delete some random comments made by bots on the Facebook wall posts, which are irrelevant to the focus of the Facebook page.
- The engagement might be strategized around just one tactic (like in Happydent). In that case the strategy should be well thought and should have a great connect with the product. However, the next strategy should be in place in case the brand notices decrease in enthusiasm amongst the fans.

10 F. Insurance (Dated: 22nd January, 2011)

Parameters	*LIC*	*HDFC Life*	*Bajaj Allianz Jiyo Befikar*
Social media widgets provided on homepage	Yes	Yes	No
Social media presence	Facebook Twitter YouTube	Facebook Twitter LinkedIn	Facebook Twitter YouTube
Facebook			
Welcome Fan tab	No	No	No
Info tab details	Yes	Yes	Yes
Integration with other social media tools	Yes	Yes	No
Community members can make post/ upload photos, videos	Yes	Yes	Yes
Applications	Customer Awareness, Unique Resolution	No	Car Insurance
Twitter			
Company name	Yes	—	No
Background image relevant to product	No	—	Yes
Location	No	—	No
Web address	Home website	—	Home website
Informative bio	No	—	Yes
YouTube			
About company	Yes	Yes (just single sentence)	No (Description about the concept, but not about company)
Video themes	TV commercials with common people as spokesperson	TV Commercials	TV Commercials

Life insurance policies are more of a necessity and is to be purchased almost by all of us to avert risks . Some of us just blindly follow the agents whom our parents trust, or sometimes consult couple of our friends to know their inputs. Once the purchase is done the interaction per se with the brand is minimal and hardly any unless you tend to decide buying another policy from the same brand. With such a unique purchase and subsequent limited interaction, an active social media presence of some of the leading insurance brands in India can be observed. In some cases, it was observed that "marketing for cause" strategy was adopted. For example Aviva created a campaign around *education* and created its presence on social media in the name of *Education is Insurance.* In this campaign, it has been emphasized that apart from academic education, these days kids need to be educated on various aspects to make them responsible human being. ICICI Prudential Life supported a cause *Living Your Passion* which encouraged the people to spend a moment from their busy life to relook and question themselves if they were engaged in activities they wanted to. However, as the focus of case studies in this book has been to study a brand's presence on social media, a detailed study of this 'cause based marketing' has not been undertaken. You are encouraged to study this unique strategy to decipher the various ways in which brands grab the customer's mindshare.

LIC *(Case Study no. 16)*

Facebook

Two Facebook pages of LIC were located on Facebook viz Life Insurance Corporation of India[1] and LIC India Forever[2]. Tracking back to the first post on both Facebook pages revealed that Life Insurance Corporation of India Facebook page was created in January, 2010 and was active till December, 2010 (till then it had 8,906 community members). The last post on this Facebook page was made on December 10, 2010 wherein it was mentioned that LIC had created the new Facebook page and they requested the community members of this page to visit the new Facebook page and "like" (the url of the new Facebook page was provided in the post) that page to remain in contact with the brand.

The LIC India Forever Facebook page was created in November,

2010 and was used recently for the engagement with 14,639 community members[3]. As the activity on new Facebook page had just picked up, in this section details of both Facebook pages have been included.

1. Life Insurance Corporation of India

The profile photo was smaller in dimension than the usual space provided by the Facebook. The Facebook page had a detailed Info section where overview, mission and products information was provided. The Facebook page was integrated with LIC's YouTube channel, and hence the community members of this page could view the videos that LIC uploaded on its YouTube channel. In the time period between September - October, 2010 LIC conducted a contest titled "Happy Family" requesting community members to upload a picture of their family for entering the contest. The photo that received the maximum likes was to be adjudged as winner on November 1, 2010. LIC made posts sharing information about the business size, premium collected etc. This could be a measure of building credibility by informing the reader of it's size of business. It was relevant from comments posted by fans that many agents, employees had been community members of this Facebook page. Sometimes these members (who were agents) provided their contact details and asked other members to contact them in case they were planning to buy any LIC policy. LIC also made posts on some products that were launched, which attracted lot of engagement from community members. However, it was noticed that LIC hardly responded to comments made by fans. From the content perspective, it was observed that LIC made judicious use of various forms of content (like photos, videos) in its posts to make it more attractive.

2. LIC India Forever

The Facebook page name was different and from the information available, it was not evident why the word "Forever" was being used. The profile photo in this Facebook page was an enhanced one compared to that of the earlier Facebook page. The reference of its entire social media presence (YouTube channel, Twitter handle, Orkut community) in the Info section[4]. Like the earlier Facebook page, this page was integrated with YouTube and Twitter, and hence facilitated community members to view tweets and videos of LIC.

With the New Year ahead, LIC conducted a contest titled "The Most Unique New Year Resolution", calling for sharing the New Year resolution in not more than 20 words. This Facebook page had a special tab "Customer Awareness Campaign"[5] wherein list of key instruction were provided to create awareness about the LIC policy guidelines. The posts made by LIC were diverse in nature. There were posts on new products, new commercials, customer awareness of services offered by LIC, news about the company (like opening up of a branch) etc. The posts made by the community members were not noticed being replied to or acknowledged by LIC and thus the level of engagement shown was low. It was surprising to see that even when fans made some queries on the Facebook page, their queries were not replied. Some fans agents tried to promote themselves by providing their contact details. This is a tricky situation as someone posting as an agent may turn out be fraud. A community member because of seeing fraud agent's details posted on the wall of the LIC page, may fall in a trap. There may be some strategy put in place to prevent such untoward incidents but the posts relating to agents were highly visible as the page was browsed at a glance.

Twitter

In LIC's Twitter handle @LICIndiaForever6, the word "Forever" was again attached behind the brand name. Like in facebook, as a person who reads it for the first time, it was not evident why this word has been used. The bio had just one sentence, *Welcome to the official twitter profile of LIC India.* It can be reflected that LIC is a household name in the country, however what about users from other countries? How would they know what LIC is? A few more details in the bio section about the company and the services offered by them could have been helpful. LIC joined Twitter in November, 2010. When this case study was written LIC's Twitter handle was *followed* by 330 *followers* and LIC *followed* 30 people. In the initial couple of months LIC just shared facts about the brand on various aspects like – brand's logo, inception of brand, number of policyholders etc. Subsequently, LIC started including link to its Facebook page in the tweets, indicating its strategy to drive better customer engagement on Facebook. LIC conducted two contests – *Revisiting Childhood* and *Unique New Year Resolutions* on its Facebook page and their tweets informing about the contests, redirected the followers to the Facebook page. The conversations happening between the brand and the followers were lacking and thus could not be noticed.

YouTube

LIC created its YouTube channel on August 30, 2010[7]. LIC used this channel majorly to promote their commercials and their sponsored events. As and when LIC came up with a new TV commercial, they uploaded that commercial on this channel. All commercials were focused on some personality or a common man who featured as a spokesperson for the brand. This concept of using common people as spokesperson in advertisements in itself could be classified as an innovative strategy. LIC had uploaded 48 videos, the channel had 129 subscribers, and total views of uploaded videos were 14,267. About 22 comments by users expressing their satisfaction after purchasing LIC policies were found on the channel.

HDFC LIFE *(Case Study no. 17)*

Facebook

When this case study was written HDFC Facebook page was in transition phase. A new Facebook page was created in January 2011[8], and fans from earlier Facebook page[9] were informed to join the new Facebook page. Two wall posts were made on earlier Facebook page informing about the new Facebook page and a web link was provided to direct fans to the new page. The new page was just started and hence the focus of this section is on the engagement activities that HDFC conducted on its earlier Facebook page.

HDFC Standard Life Insurance[10]

The posts made by HDFC on this earlier Facebook page had a photo or a video content attached to it. When HDFC Life created its YouTube channel, it was shared on its wall. The wall posts were also on awards what HDFC achieved for its product, for being best employer etc. The posts on some media coverage of the brand were also shared on the wall along with the link to the news. The interviews of senior executives of the brand that were uploaded on YouTube channel of HDFC were too shared here. Though this Facebook page was created in January, 2010; the frequency of posts made on wall was quite low and it may be one of the reasons that Facebook page couldn't attract large number of fans. The Facebook page had about 770 community members by the end of the year and with the rebranding event, HDFC had to now shift to another Facebook page. It's always an uphill task to regain members. Another reason for this low number could be the lack of engagement as the comments made by fan were rarely replied or acknowledged by the brand.

Twitter

The Twitter handle for HDFC Life was @HDFCLife[11]. The Twitter handle image was very small and users might face difficulty noticing it. The home website was provided in the Web section and a straight forward message was provided in the Bio section indicating that it was the official Twitter handle. HDFC Life created its Twitter handle on 25th February, 2010 and seemed to have discontinued using this Twitter handle as the last tweet on its handle was on 18th August, 2010[12]. HDFC Life used Twitter mainly to inform its followers about new products that were introduced and also tried to handle grievances through this channel.

LinkedIn

HDFC Life had created its LinkedIn page as HDFC Standard Life Insurance[13].The page had 2152 followers, which included 2,130 employees[14]. When a user visits the LinkedIn page he/she could see how many members from his/her network (1st level and 2nd level connections) were members of this LinkedIn page. The key features of the LinkedIn page which include *key statistics, company description, company employees, new hires, recent promotions and changes, popular profiles*[15] would help members reach the right person in case of need. LinkedIn pages also help firms in branding their employees.

BAJAJ ALLIANZ *(Case Study no. 18)*

Facebook

The Facebook page of Bajaj Allianz was named as *Jiyo Befikar*[16] (which in English means live without worries), which was the tagline of the brand. The profile picture was too a shot taken from its TV commercial, which symbolized the tagline of the brand. The Facebook page had the special tab *Car Insurance.* When the message (Calculate

Your Car Insurance Premium in Just 15 seconds!)[17] on this tab was clicked, it directed to the home website of the brand where the calculator is available for users to calculate the premium for their car on their own. Bajaj Allianz had a detailed Info section; information on the products could not be located as was in the case of the other two brands mentioned in this section. The wall posts by Bajaj were informative in nature which included some tips for customers. The wall posts had a weblink attached to them, which redirected to an appropriate webpage on the Bajaj Allianz website which had the relevant information. The strategy to redirect the user to a source of detailed content was adopted. This helps customers to have better details on the topic. Bajaj was very active in engaging with the fans. It could be observed that the brand was promptly interacting and responding to the comments on a regular basis. The tone of wall post text was very friendly and suggestive in nature and it appeared as if one is advising a friend to visit the attached weblink to get a particular task done in an appropriate manner. Such tone helps build closer connect with the community members rather than having a very professional contact with them.

Twitter

The Twitter handle for Bajaj Allianz was @Jiyobefikar[18]. The Twitter background and the Twitter handle image consisted of a scene from one of its TV commercial. The home website address as provided in the Web section and the description of the *Jiyo Befikar* concept was written in the Bio section. Bajaj Allianz as and when this case study was written seems to have stopped using this channel as part of their social media strategy as there were only 26 tweets made from this handle and the last tweet on its Twitter handle on July 29th, 2009[19]. For the short time during which they tweeted, most of their tweets were about the campaign they ran in line with Hindi movie "Love Aaj Kal" that was released during that time. The last tweet was a very direct sales pitch which said *Buy online insurance*[20].

YouTube

Bajaj Allianz (Jiyo Befikar) created its YouTube channel on June 4, 2009[21]. Maintaining consistency with other social media channels the name of the channel has been maintained as *Jiyo* Befikar here too. Atleast on Facebook page the info section had details that clearly indicated that this Facebook page was owned by Bajaj Allianz. However this wasn't indicated in Twitter and YouTube. Even in the "About Me" section the firm didn't give any indication of its brand name, which might be in some cases risky, as not all visitors to the channel might be aware of the message (*Jiyo Befikar)* and they might not relate it to the brand name. Bajaj Allianz leveraged its TV commercials as the major source of content for their YouTube channel. As and when a new TV commercial was launched, it was uploaded on this channel. As when this chapter was written, Bajaj Allianz had uploaded just 23 videos, the channel had 26 subscribers, and total views of uploaded videos were 27,832[22]. The comments on this channel showed appreciation towards the quality of commercials.

Insights & Observations:

- It should be kept in mind that, any social network user residing in any part of the world might land on your Facebook page or Twitter handle. At that time the user should get enough information about the brand and should not be required to search the company's website to get information. Hence, the Info section on Facebook page, Bio section in Twitter, Profile section in YouTube & Blog should be very carefully written and should provide as much comprehensive information as possible.
- The user name of a Facebook page, Twitter handle or YouTube channel is the first and most important contact to the community member who visits it for the first time. If the user name is something other than the brand name, the community member would need to put in extra effort to search for additional information about the reliability of that particular channel. This additional effort required might deter some users to make use of this channel. Hence, to avoid such instances it would be advisable to have a detailed section about the identity of the brand at the respective place on the channel – for instance in the Info section of Facebook page, Bio section of Twitter handle, About me section of YouTube channel etc.
- The brands need to make effort to engage with fans by responding to comments made by them. Just making posts

and not responding to comments might send negative vibes to the fans, and could lower the engagement level on the Facebook page.

- The promotional messages by distributors, retailers, salespeople on the brand's Facebook page should not be entertained by brand and its brands responsibility to avoid such behavior, as it might be irritating for community members. The Facebook page should be utilized primarily for engaging with their brand and such sales pitches should be filtered.
- In case there is change in the brand name, the existing Facebook page cannot be renamed (as it is not encouraged by Facebook regulations). Hence, a new Facebook page needs to be created, and brands should take special efforts for directing community members to the new Facebook page, else they would never know about the new Facebook page and brand might lose engagement with them.
- It would be an attractive strategy to redirect fans to a detailed content source, either on the brand's website or a reputed blog or brand's blog wherein the user can gain in-depth information.
- Insurance being a high involvement product, i.e. customer spending lot of time in evaluating products offered by various players in the market, it was observed that customer engagement on social media was centered around: building brand reputation in the minds of community members, sharing achievements of brands, providing tips on various service aspects, building credibility about products etc. The content hence was informative in nature and usually avoided humor. It also relied heavily on contests oriented, polls oriented etc. This difference in content execution adapted to each situation needs to be understood and accordingly implemented.

10 G. Airlines (Dated: 24th January, 2011)

Parameters	*Jet Airways*	*Kingfisher Airlines*	*SpiceJet Airlines*
Social media widgets provided on homepage	Yes	Yes	No
Social media presence	Facebook Twitter YouTube Flickr	Facebook Twitter	Facebook Twitter YouTube
Facebook			
Welcome Fan tab	No	No	Yes
Info tab details	Yes	Yes	Yes
Integration with other social media tools	Yes (Only with Twitter)	No	No
Community members can make post/ upload photos, videos	No	Yes	Yes
Applications	Jet Airways Book Flights	Events	Book a Flight
Twitter			
Company name	Yes	Yes	Yes
Background image relevant to product	Yes	Yes	Yes
Location	India	India	Gurgaon
Web address	Home website	Home website	Feedback webpage on home website
Informative bio	Yes	Yes	Yes
YouTube			
About company	No	—	Yes
Video themes	TV commercials	—	TV Commercials

The low cost carriers almost redefined the Indian aviation industry by competing directly with the first class railway fares and thus fulfilling the Indian middle class dream to *'fly'*. In a price sensitive market like India, there exists substantial difference in fares between full service (like Indian Airlines, Kingfisher, Jet Airways) and low cost carriers. Even amongst both sub categories (full service, low cost) the difference in value proposition can be observed across the value chain right from booking tickets, updating passengers about flight timings, handling baggage, providing special check-in facility, providing facility to select desired seats etc. The cut throat competition in the industry for offering a superior service in stringent cost constraints makes it imperative to build a favourable brand image among the existing and prospective customers. The social media initiatives undertaken by three brands in the industry to build engagement with the customers are discussed in this section.

JET AIRWAYS *(Case Study no. 19)*

Facebook

The Facebook page of Jet Airways[1] had a detailed Info section, where all details about the brand were provided. The introduction of other two subsidiary brands Jet Airways Konnect and JetLite was also included in the Info section. Jet Airways had two applications on its Facebook Page – "Jet Airways" and "Book Flights". The Jet Airways application had reference to facilities like online booking, web check-in, flight status, etc. Any community member, who wished to have additional information on them, could click on it and he/she would be directed to the relevant webpage on the home website. The Book Flights application had search facility for users to find flight for booking. When community members would click on the search tab, the user would be directed to the webpage of the Jet Airways where the entire booking process could be accomplished. This can be noted as an innovative strategy of directing the traffic from the Facebook page and which may ultimately result in a sale.

Jet Airways made extensive use of photos while making posts on its wall, 113 photos were used as and when this case study was written[2]. Use of relevant photos in wall posts created a special appeal. The detailed discussion posts, press releases were shared in Notes section, which attracted engagement from the community members.

The community members didn't have access to make posts on the wall; it was only the brand which could make posts. The wall posts made by brand were focused on in-flight entertainment facilities, facts about tourists destinations, flying tips, promotional offers, flight details, updates on important events that were scheduled at destinations (to which Jet Airways had flight connectivity) etc. It was observed that despite just reinforcing the brand time and again, Jet Airways engaged with community members on a wide number of topics and kept them engaged. Jet Airways interacted with community members and responded to their comments in an apt manner.

Twitter

The Twitter handle of Jet Airways was @jetairways[3]. The Twitter handle had all elements in right shape – an attractive and relevant Twitter background which had a welcome message *Welcome abroad Jet Airways. India's premier international airline*, and had reference to its Facebook Page and Twitter handle; the brand logo was used as the Twitter handle image; detailed Twitter bio which emphasized that brand was present here to converse with the community members; and finally the home website was referred. The conversations on this handle had a significant amount of variety viz. providing support to community members in using mobile apps, handling customer grievances, loyalty schemes, online booking, food quality served on flight, baggage handling etc. It was observed that Jet Airways exhibited humility while dealing with all grievances and assured that steps would be taken to correct them in future. The community members were also encouraged by Jet Airways to write a detailed email to the respective departments and emails for the same were provided. For example guestrelations@jetairways.com (for queries on general services), baggageservices@jetairways.com (for queries related on baggage handling), dxbreservations@jetairways.com (for queries on reservations) etc. Some tweets from the brand were on some added service, a few facts about certain destinations (brand made use of hashtag #JetFacts), provided some tips on travel (with the use of hashtag #JetTips), special offers that were announced (with the use of hashtag #JetDeals), security arrangements at some airports etc. Twitter handle was used mainly to listen to customers and brand got less engaged in "broadcasting". The Twitter handle acted as a central place to collect all conversations and each query was directed to the respective department for further action. This indicates the well coordinated integration between departments. The need for this seamless integration between the departments and social media channels has been emphasized in the social media strategy chapter no. 6 of this book.

YouTube

Jet Airways created its YouTube channel on August 17, 2006[4]. Jet Airways used this channel majorly to promote their TV commercials. As and when Jet Airways came up with a new TV commercial, they uploaded that commercial on this channel. The commercials highlighted the premium services offered by Jet Airways like web check-in, unique experience etc. Jet Airways had uploaded 8 videos, the channel had 34 subscribers, and total views of uploaded videos were 1,349[5]. When this case study was written just 4 comments were found on the channel. In these comments, the customers had expressed their satisfaction with the services offered by Jet Airways.

Flickr

Jet Airways created its photostream on Flickr in January, 2011[6]. Jet Airways uploaded 200 photos on January 10, 2011[7]. The photos were about various offline events that Jet Airways conducted to build connect with stakeholders. No engagement or interaction could be noticed on this channel. One of the possible reasons could be its recent launch. In order to garner engagement on Flickr, one of the steps could be sharing this link on Facebook. This was not noticed when this case study was written.

KINGFISHER AIRLINES *(Case Study no. 20)*

Facebook

The Facebook page of Kingfisher was named as FlyKingfisher[8]. The brand logo was used for the Facebook profile image. The Info section had detailed information about the company, mission, services offered, social media presence and website. Kingfisher Airlines didn't have a YouTube channel for its airlines service, but had a corporate YouTube channel *KingofGoodTimes*[9]. The posts on wall focussed on package offers, quizzes, information on tourist destinations, contests, etc. The wall posts on information about tourist destinations had weblinks which directed the user to a special Kingfisher website named as Kingfisher Holidays[10]. This website had all information about both domestic and international destinations and tour packages. Apart from the brand, even community managers made wall posts; sometimes they even uploaded photos from real life experiences and shared it with other community members. Kingfisher was forthcoming enough to engage with enthusiastic community members by commenting on their wall posts.

Twitter

The Twitter handle of Kingfisher Airlines was @flykingfisher[11]. Kingfisher had an informative bio wherein it clearly shared the objective of this Twitter handle and purpose for which they created this presence. The Twitter background had the brand logo repeated several times across the screen. Kingfisher ran contests on this Twitter handle like identifying a destination, ideal destination in user's city for weekend party (which was named as "Splendid Weekend" contest, and was meant for community members from various cities like Mumbai, Kolkatta, Delhi, Pune, Goa etc,) etc. At regular intervals Kingfisher also tweeted various offers that were available for customers. Apart from this Kingfisher had engagement with community members on queries raised by them regarding booking, flight journey, on-ground services, gifts for contests etc. Kingfisher like Jet Airways had interaction with its community members on a variety of topics, which could be a good strategy to sustain engagement on a long term.

SPICEJET AIRLINES *(Case Study no. 21)*

Facebook

The image on Facebook page was that of SpiceJet flight in the sky[12]. The Info section had just a single sentence indicating that "SpiceJet is the most preferred low fare airline", which delivered high value to customers. SpiceJet had an attractive Welcome tab in which were also include links to offers. When this case study was written a contest was floated to community members, which called for listing sights and places to visit in Pune. This was also included in the Welcome tab. It was noted that SpiceJet didn't make any post on its wall. Also there was lack of interaction happening on the wall.

The Facebook page was created in February 2010 and until this case was written, not even a single post was made by brand. A few posts were made on wall by community members, some of them expressing their satisfaction towards the services offered, while some expressed their grievances. The brand didn't respond to any of the wall posts. It is not a common practice to see a brand creating a Facebook page and not making a wall post since almost one year or even responding to wall posts that were made by community members.

Twitter

The Twitter handle was named as @flyspicejet[13] similar to that of Kingfisher airlines. The Twitter background was plain red in colour (symbolizing the brand's identity) with the brand name and slogan at top left corner in the vertical position. The Twitter bio indicated that it is a low fare airline and it flew to 22 destinations across India, Nepal and Sri Lanka and operated 169 daily flights[14]. The web address of feedback webpage on SpiceJet's home website was provided and Gurgaon (their corporate headquarters location) was mentioned in the location tab. SpiceJet Twitter handle had hardly any interaction. Almost all tweets were about an offer, with a standard message format – *Fly <Destination A> to <Destination B> starting from Rs. <X> for travel <Y> date onwards!* The tweets did not symbolize a personal connect and appeared as a broadcasted message. It was noticed that Hootsuite social media dashboard was used prominently, which gave an impression that maybe tweets were scheduled through the dashboard the broadcasting of tweets was mechanized instead of a person tweeting them live). No other interaction was visible on the Twitter handle, at as and when this case study was written.

YouTube

SpiceJet's created its YouTube channel named as *The Official SpiceJet Channel*[15] on October 19, 2009[16]. SpiceJet used this channel mainly to promote their TV commercials. As and when Spicejet came up with a new TV commercial, they uploaded that commercial on this channel. The commercials highlighted web check-in, in-flight food service, unique experience, and timely flight operations offered by SpiceJet. As and when this chapter was written, SpiceJet had uploaded 10 videos, the channel had 37 subscribers, and total views of uploaded videos were 32,201[17]. When this case study was written just 6 comments were found on the channel, with some customers expressing their satisfaction towards services offered by SpiceJet, their liking for TV commercials etc.

Insights & Observations:

- The use of interactive applications on social media channel helps engaging the community members in an entertaining manner.
- Contests run for specific cities could help brand gain more focused target audience and also motivate community members from those cities to actively get engage with the brand. This might cause a few more users from those cities to like Facebook page or follow the brand on Twitter.
- Sustaining engagement can be suitable if various activities relevant to the customer's purchase and service aspects are kept active on a channel.
- Brands should avoid broadcasting messages through social media dashboards by scheduling tweets. Scheduling tweets should help in case brand is operating in multiple timelines, however it should be used with care, else the user reading such tweets would easily notice the lack of personal touch in them.
- When community members make wall posts on Facebook or express their experiences with brand on Twitter, YouTube etc. brands should make an effort to engage with such users. Engagement could be as simple as thanking them for their positive words, or assuring them of better service next time (in case of grievances), or offering a help at the earliest.

10 H. Multiplexes (Dated: 25th January, 2011)

Parameters	*PVR Cinemas*	*BIG Cinemas*	*Inox Leisure*
Social media widgets provided on homepage	No	Yes	Yes
Social media presence	Facebook Twitter YouTube	Facebook YouTube	Facebook Twitter
Facebook			
Welcome Fan tab	No	Yes	No
Info tab details	Yes	Yes	Yes
Integration with other social media tools	No	No	No
Community members can make post/ upload photos, videos	Yes	Yes	Yes
Applications	Book Movie	Events 3+1 Offer Vote here! Reviews House Rules	Reviews
Twitter			
Company name	Yes	Yes	Yes
Background image relevant to product	Yes	Yes	Yes
Location	India	India	Gurgaon
Web address	Home website	Home website	Home website
Informative bio	Yes	Yes	Yes
YouTube			
About company	Yes	Yes	Yes
Video themes	Movie trailers	Movie trailers, Customer service, Podcast	TV Commercials

Its often said that movies and cricket sells easily in India. Indians are well known across the world for passion of cinema. Unless and until it's movie of an all time favourite superstar, the days when people used to wait in long queues outside single screen movie theatres or buy tickets in black market (sometimes at double the rates) are a thing of the past. The advent and subsequent growth of multiplexes in India has changed the 'movie' experience to 'movie+ shopping +food' experience and beyond. The multiplexes are often bundled with shopping destinations and food joints which in total make a complete package for family to spend their time together on weekends and holidays. Multiplexes also have given a variety of choice to the movie goers including English movies which were once considered to be luxury. Multiplexes launched innovative services like ticket booking via phone, SMS, Internet etc., and also providing snacks services right at the seat, choice to select a seat etc. Some of the major players in this industry are PVR Cinemas, BIG Cinemas, DT Cinemas, Inox, etc. Movie is such a product category wherein multiplexes do not have the main role to play to decide the 'purchase intention' of which movie to watch. Movie decisions are most often made based on the starcast, storyline and the word of mouth. However, once the decision to watch the movie has been made, it's quintessential for multiplex brands to be a 'top of the mind' recall for the movie-goer. The social media journey of three leading multiplex brands has been discussed in this section

PVR CINEMAS *(Case Study no. 22)*

Facebook

PVR Cinemas had its brand logo as the Facebook profile picture. The info section was detailed with all information about its national presence[1] (number of screens and list of all cities). PVR Cinemas often made use of photos in the wall posts, which was evident from large number of photos on their Photos section that had 18 albums[2]. The wall posts mostly focused on movie reviews along with images from that movie. It was observed that PVR Cinemas asked for small review or rating of movie through their wall posts from the community members. This elicited decent and sometimes a warm response from the community members. Sometimes, videos of movie trailers were also shared from PVR's YouTube channel. PVR also made wall posts with the tone of quiz wherein an incomplete sentence was provided to judge the community member's inclination towards the movie. A few times wall posts were made on dialogues from movie and community members were asked to judge the movie. On the whole, it was noticed that engagement on this Facebook page was positioned around movies with some quizzes used to obtain responses and participation from the community members. Building the engagement around the core offering (movies in this case) was well thought out and executed strategy. Interestingly, the brand hardly offered any gifts to the winners, however the enthusiasm of community members was high enough and such open ended question format in quizzes attract lot of participation. This once again reinforces that 'recognition' is taking preference over 'rewards in the minds of people especially the young generation.

When a user would search for PVR in Facebook, the search results also showed an application[3] by PVR Cinemas. The application however, was not integrated with the PVR Cinemas Facebook page. The application provided the complete experience of a website and a user could browse through the movies, search for locations, and book the tickets right there on the application itself. The user doesn't have to visit the website at all for any purpose; the entire ticket booking process could be completed on the application itself. This helped user to complete the transaction without getting directed away from facebook.

Twitter

The Twitter handle of PVR Cinemas was @_PVRCinemas[4]. The Twitter background has the image of brand logo and the reference of PVR's YouTube channel, Facebook page, and helpline number. The reference of home website is provided in the Web section and a single sentence *India's leading Cinema Chain* is included in the Bio section[5]. PVR cinema tweeted with comparatively less frequency and updated its followers about movie releases, when online booking was available for upcoming movies. PVR also interacted with followers who had tagged the brand for certain query. It was noticed that PVR also engaged with a few Bollywood stars like Minissha Lamba (@Minissha_Lamba), Vivek Oberoi (@vivek_oberoi), Uday Chopra (@udaychopra), Arbaaz Khan (@arbaazSkhan), etc.

YouTube

PVR Cinemas created its YouTube channel on June 10, 2010[6]. Both Hollywood and Bollywood movie trailers were uploaded on this channel. As and when this case study was written, PVR cinemas had uploaded 38 videos, the channel had 38 subscribers, and total views of uploaded videos were 8,090[7]. Though it was observed that subscribers did views these videos, there was just one comment made. It was noticed that PVR cinemas had subscribed to UTV Motion Picture's and Reliance Big Cinema's YouTube channels. This could be good strategy to keep a track on competition, so that creative ideas can be generated and trends observed for implementation in one's own channel. Also it can help in branding as those who subscribe to any of the competitors may also see PVR there and they may subscribe to PVR as well.

BIG CINEMAS *(Case Study no. 23)*

Facebook

The Facebook page of BIG Cinemas was named as *BIG Cinemas India*[8]. When this case study was written, the profile image depicted a message related to a contest *Fans Choice 2011,* which was to begin on February 1, 2011. The Info section was detailed in all aspects – website, company overview, products, mission, about etc. The Events tab had the list of events that were conducted by BIG Cinemas on Facebook page. The *3 + 1 Offer* tab provides information about the promotional offer, wherein BIG Cinemas gave a free ticket for weekday movie, for every 3 weekend movie tickets. The community members could give ratings for a movie in the Reviews tab, where the community member could click on the rating scale and write the name of the movie, for which they were expressing their views[9]. The House Rules tab had clear instruction to community members about maintaining discipline on the Facebook page, and it explicitly made it clear that any personal attacks, vulgar messages or racist comments would not be entertained and they would be immediately deleted. This was an interesting feature, which clearly defined the rules of engagement. The Vote Here! tab had a few questions for e.g. preferred time slot to watch movie, preferred mode of booking tickets etc. to which users were supposed to vote. Around 400 people gave votes to these questions[10].

Photos were extensively used by BIG Cinemas on their wall photos, which was evident from the fact that about 97 albums existed in their Photos section[11]. Photos from the BIG Cinemas theatres were captured and shared on the wall, probably to give a look and feel about their place to the community members. BIG Cinemas ran various contests, and gave free movie tickets to the winners. The most common contest strategy followed by BIG Cinemas was to request community members to tag their friends on the images that BIG Cinemas included in a wall post. BIG Cinemas also conducted offline events and shared those live experiences on wall along with the photos. BIG Cinemas shared video content in the form of movie trailers. As the wall was open for community members to post, some community members had expressed their grievances having not received their gifts, after they won at contests. BIG Cinemas responded to some of them, but a significant number were left unattended. It may be possible that a private message was sent to them or the discussion taken offline. On the whole, it could be said that major attraction of this brand community was contests, and community members were rewarded with movie tickets for the efforts they put in to participate in the contests.

YouTube

BIG Cinemas created its YouTube channel on May 23, 2010[12]. BIG Cinemas had a customized YouTube channel background with scenes from Bollywood movies. Apart from Hollywood and Bollywood movie trailers BIG Cinemas also had a video demonstrating on how to claim prize from their website and offline. A campaign was run which consisted of ten videos wherein an employee acted as a spy of the organization and he updated the viewers of the YouTube channel about the steps that BIG Cinema was taking. This was an interesting move, as instead of sharing the message directly with the viewers, the concept of maintaining the suspense over a period of ten videos and framing the content, as if some employee is spying is a surprise value. As and when this chapter was written, BIG cinemas had uploaded 34 videos, the channel had 34 subscribers, and total views of uploaded videos were 26,689[13] (much higher than that of PVR cinemas). Though it was observed that subscribers did view these videos, there were no comments made by the subscribers. It was noticed that BIG cinemas had subscribed to UTV Motion Picture's, Eros Entertainment, Yash Raj Films, Studio 18, PVR Cinema's YouTube channels[14]. This was a similar strategy as followed by PVR cinemas too.

INOX LEISURE *(Case Study no. 24)*

Facebook

The Facebook page of Inox was named as Inox Leisure Ltd.[15]. The brand logo was used as the profile image and a detailed description about company, mission, and products provided in the Info section. It was observed that the major content strategy followed by Inox included movie release information (in all languages) provided early in the week of scheduled relase, either on Monday or Tuesday (probably providing customers sufficient time to decide on their weekend plans), offline event intimations, movie trailers and contests. Inox made extensive use of photos and videos in their wall posts that suited the message. It was noticed that various contests were conducted at regular intervals of time, mostly based on movies, sometimes community members were asked to mail (facebook@inox.co.in) their first show tickets, etc. Community members regularly participated and Inox too responded to their comments as and when required. Apart from Inox's wall posts, community members also made wall posts and it was observed that users generally had queries regarding movie releases in their city, receiving contest gifts, opening of new screens in their city etc. Also, a few community members made daily greetings wall posts like good morning, good afternoon etc. The community members also made use of Discussions section, where they expressed their thoughts and initiated discussions, however hardly any engagement was seen on those discussion posts. Like BIG Cinema, Inox too had the Reviews application, wherein community members could express their ratings for a movie.

Twitter

The Twitter handle of Inox was @InoxLeisure[16]. The Twitter background has multiple features – brand logo; reference to website, sms, gprs, Facebook page; images of Inox multiplexes (which gave the viewer a feel of its infrastructure). The Bio mentioned, "*LIVE THE MOVIE only at INOX, India's favourite movie destination*".

The tweets focused on movie release information (similar to that of their wall posts on their Facebook page), information on special preview screenings, birthday wishes to Bollywood & Hollywood actors and actresses, etc. The frequency of tweets was hardly one or two per day. The engagement was to limited extent on the Twitter handle, and it was mostly a one directional broadcasting. The duplication of movie release information on Twitter and Facebook page probably couldn't provide space for engagement on the Twitter handle.

Insights & Observations:

- The central object of engagement related to a brand can be tactfully handled through various ways like quizzes, contests, polls etc. However, deciding what should be this central object needs to be well thought and should be held on to justify the community which is built around a brand.
- In recent times it has been observed that brands have shown interest to provide shopping experience on the Facebook page with the help of applications. These applications provide complete purchase experience and user doesn't have to visit the website for any purpose.
- Whether to run contests based on incentives or without incentives would be a key decision that brands need to take. It is not necessary that all brands need to offer monetary or material incentives. There can be a 'recognition' incentive based strategy also. The award or incentive based strategy needs to be based on their overall value proposition and the way it is being received by the customers.
- When same message is used to engage with community members on two different social media channels, it may so happen that community members might choose one channel over the other (in most cases the one that is more convenient to them). If the brand has a specific positioning for using a particular social channel, it should make sure that is reflected as distinct by the way it sends out messages, rather than just sending the same message across without any adaptation.
- Use of applications should be made in an appropriate way such that it should have close match with the product category and the consumer behaviour towards that product.

10 I. Apparels (Dated: 27th January, 2011)

Parameters	*Indian Terrain*	*Pantaloons*	*Teesort*
Social media widgets provided on homepage	Yes	Yes	Yes
Social media presence	Facebook YouTube	Facebook Twitter YouTube	Facebook Twitter Blog, Orkut
Facebook			
Welcome Fan tab	No	No	No
Info tab details	Yes	Yes	Yes
Integration with other social media tools	No	No	No
Community members can make post/ upload photos, videos	Yes	Yes	Yes
Applications	Ambassadors Browse Make	SALE Style inc 2.0 CEO Wall of Fame Store Locator Livestream Gifting Special Offers Events	Teezzle Email Signup TS Vote TS Quiz
Twitter			
Company name	—	Yes	Yes
Background image relevant to product	—	Yes	Yes
Location	—	India	New Delhi
Web address	—	Facebook page	Home website
Informative bio	—	Yes	Yes

YouTube			
About company	No	No	—
Video themes	TV Commercials	TV Commercials Offline events	—
Blog			
About blog	—	—	Yes
Blog post categories	—	—	Yes
Archives	—	—	Yes
Search facility	—	—	No

Apparel is one category where Indians are known to spend generously . Even occasions like a friend's marriage, family get together etc is considered to be a reason to spend enough on apparels. The opening of Indian markets lead to a flurry of foreign brands with ready-to-wear products causing a considerable shift from customized stitched apparels. Apart from the branded products, in recent times it could be noticed that many local brands have tried to capture market share in the crowded industry, thanks to the lower manufacturing costs and cheaper online retailing options. It is no longer essential for manufacturers to have their retail 'brick and mortar' outlets. In as less as a few thousand rupees they can set up an online shop, and with the increasing confidence of Indian consumers in e-commerce, there are good chances of success. Now, with the social media these so-called 'local brands' have the potential to become large reasonably fast. In this section, social media journey of two established apparel players and one relatively new comer is discussed.

INDIAN TERRAIN *(Case Study no. 25)*

Facebook

The Facebook page of Indian Terrain was named as *Indian Terrian*[1]. In the Info section, brand had mentioned the following message, "*Its about wearing clothes you are comfortable in. Its about the attitude that you exude by doing whatever it is you do. Justbe*"[2]. Any other information to introduce the brand wasn't available in the Info section. Apart from the regular wall posts on weekend sale, special offers, brand also engaged with community members by involving them in conversations related to their life, for e.g. *What was your OMG moment this weekend?*[3], *People usually do something fun on the weekend. What did you do this weekend?*[4], *So how many people are on Facebook from work?*[5] etc. The brand also shared news related to the brand (like availability in some other countries), sponsorships that the brand was involved for an offline event. As the wall was open for community members to make posts, many community members used it for variety of purposes like queries for offers in a specific store nearby their residence, inquiring about price for a product, shared images of their brand's possessions (this act happened often, leading to lot of image collection on the Facebook page), expressed their satisfaction with the newly bought product from the brand etc. The brand replied to such wall posts comprehensively, exhibiting that brand was listening to its community members. The Facebook page also had couple of applications – 'Ambassadors', 'Browse Make'. The names of community members of the Facebook page who actively participated (made status updates about brand on their wall, shared images about brand, shared stories how small changes impacted their life) in the community, were listed (along with the criteria for which they were selected) in the Ambassadors application[6]. This strategy utilized the 'recognition' need of the user well by not only identifying the key influencers from brand's community, but also appreciating their efforts on the same stage. The Browse Make application had small contests which directed the user to the brand's home website, wherein the user had to participate in the contest.

YouTube

Indian Terrain created its YouTube channel on October 16, 2009[7] and it was named *ChangewithIT*. As and when this case study was written the brand had uploaded just one video, which was its TV commercial. This video had total upload views of 326[8] and no one subscribed to its channel. It was clearly indicative this social media channel wasn't actively used by brand, but it was unclear why did brand make it visible on its homepage.

PANTALOONS *(Case Study no. 26)*

Facebook

The Facebook page was named as Pantaloons[9] and had a comprehensive profile image, which incorporated its brand logo, social media presence indications and the sale message. The Info section had most of the information about Pantaloons, right from when the brand was found, the mission, the value proposition offered, online shopping website address etc. Pantaloons made use of many applications on its Facebook page, some of the prominent ones were Store locator, CEO Wall of Fame, Style Inc 2.0, Gifting, Livestream etc. Pantaloons regularly updated the Events application, with all details of the offline event, in which the brand participated as sponsor. Pantaloons also used Notes section to share some detailed information about various topics, which led to engagement. Pantaloon's wall posts mainly focused on offers, and they included attractive images along with the wall posts, which is very essential for the kind of product category they were in. They also ran various contests like asking community members to click their photographs with the shopping bag, complete the sentence, apart from various other open ended quizzes on wardrobe selection, fashion, new style etc. Every wall post attracted hundreds of *likes* and substantial number of comments. The use of attractive images of models adorning latest offering added a unique feel to the Facebook page, which was relevant for the brand, given the value proposition and product category it was involved with. Pantaloons had 188 photo albums (as and when this case study was written[10]) and about 415 photos were uploaded by community members, which indicated enormous engagement by the community members. The conversations however mostly sustained around the apparels, fashion, etc. The community members also expressed their satisfaction, liking towards the brand, some of them inquired about offers, etc. on the wall, to which brand responded (replied) effectively.

Twitter

The Twitter handle of Pantaloons was @pantaloonsindia[11]. The Twitter background was customized and had an image of a female model. The Twitter handle image had a combination of brand logo and a female model. The Bio - *Pantaloons offers trendy and hip fashion wear with a focus on the youth of today*[12] describes the brand and what it offers. The Web section had reference to brand's Facebook page and not the home website, as usually brands provide, which displayed the confidence and commitment the brand had on the Facebook page. Pantaloons primarily used this handle to update its followers about new fashion that arrived at stores. Pantaloons made extensive use of Twitpic[13] application, to upload images along with their tweets. In this manner Pantaloons made an attempt to keep the attention of the users at Twitter itself, instead of redirecting the users to any other social media channel to access the images. A standard tweet format was noticed – "#Fashion Flashback <url>", which was tweeted often. Sometimes, Pantaloons included the Twitter handle of models that were displayed in the images. Pantaloons located all tweets that mentioned the brand and 'retweeted' them, thus further stimulating the engagement. Pantaloons also tweeted about the specific offers, offerings that were available at a specific city to involve Twitter users from these cities to follow the brand. This strategy capitalized on the potential of 'localization'.

YouTube

Pantaloons India's YouTube channel was created on May 16, 2009 and was named as PantaloonsFashion[14]. Pantaloons had a customized YouTube channel background with images of female models adorning the brand offerings. The videos uploaded on the channel were focused on TV commercials and offline events which Pantaloons had sponsored (mainly videos from Miss India contest were uploaded), fashion shows etc. Videos of interview with Miss India contestants, interaction of Facebook page contest winners with Miss India contestants etc. were uploaded on this channel. One of the videos[15] about a CXO's visit to a Pune store was in Marathi language which showed representation of vernacular. As and when this chapter was written, Pantaloons had uploaded 49 videos, the channel had 33 subscribers, and total views of uploaded videos were 68,589[16] (much higher than that of PVR cinemas). Pantaloons seemed to be using this channel majorly to highlight the fashion element and maintain *cool* quotient amongst its customers.

TEESORT *(Case Study no. 27)*

Teesort is an online retail brand for T-shirts[17] founded in 2010. They offer a unique value proposition of bringing both designers and customers on a same channel. The designers can design creative T-shirts and gain rewards (which includes profit sharing too) and customers can buy T-shirts with those creative designs printed on them18.

Facebook

The Facebook page was named as teesort.com[19]. The profile image used (as and when this case study was written) was a customized image for the Republic day with the brand name and slogan. The Info section had all details about the brand which included detailed company overview, mission, location, social media presence, email, etc. Teesort primarily used the Facebook page to receive feedback on latest designs by designers and to share the news with the community about the brand. These wall posts included an image and a weblink to the blogpost wherein the details about the design was provided. Hence, the user was redirected from the wall post to the blogpost. Also, Teesort made due efforts to tag the designer on the wall post, which is a great sign of accrediting the efforts of the designer amongst the community members, and also creating an opportunity for the designer as anyone interested in a similar assignment might contact the designer directly. This was a unique approach, which was unusual in the traditional apparels business, where customer would seldom know who designed a particular design and rarely had the chance to interact with the designer. Starting from August, 2010 in the beginning of every month, Teesort shared a set of designs as that month's collection. However, apart from the brand related conversations, Teesort also engaged the community members with news from current affairs; short quizzes on sports, general knowledge etc.; puzzles; discussions on movies; wished Bollywood personalities on their birthday; quizzes based on cropped images of Bollywood stars, etc. Teesort also made use of interesting applications like Teezzle, Email Signup, TS Vote, TS Quiz on the Facebook page. Teezzle application had four puzzles[20] which community members could play around. The Email Signup[21], application had the form to be filled in by the community members to receive newsletter from Teesort. The TS Vote[22] application had various T-shirt designs which were uploaded regularly by the brand and the community members had to vote them on a scale of 1 to 5 to express their likings. TS Quiz[23] application had a quiz which community members could participate in to know their personality. Overall strategy of Teesort has been to maintain the *cool* quotient on its Facebook and use of innovative applications helped it significantly to sustain engagement.

Twitter

The Twitter handle of Teesort was @Teesort[24]. The Twitter handle had a well-designed creative background, with references of its Twitter handle and Facebook page, Email, Phone, Address. The Bio section had enough details about the brand's value proposition for designers and customers. The Bio section also included the specific message about the Facebook page – *Also join us on www.facebook.com/teesort for contests.* The message conveyed through tweets was same as those of wall posts on Facebook page. The links provided in the tweets either directed the followers to Facebook wall post or to the blogpost on the Teesort blog. No specific content strategy specific to Twitter channel was found, mainly it was used as a means to redirect the followers to the Facebook page and blog.

Blog

The Teesort blog was named as *The Teesort Blogsville*[25]. The blog was well designed and guided the first time visitor with well defined tabs – About us, New Arrivals, Videos, Contests, Contact us. Also, the blogpost categories had a dropdown menu wherein categories like About us, Cricket Mania, Fashionista, In the Limelight, New Arrivals, Our Latest Contest, Videos Teesort were listed. The blogposts in the About us category[26] were written in the month of May-June, 2010 and had details about the brand, the concept, the value proposition they offered etc. The blogposts in the Cricket Mania category[27] was written in the month of May, 2010, had contests in-built in them and rewards were announced for the winners. The blogposts in the Fashionista category[28] were written in the month of September, 2010, and had focus on fashion quotient of the T-shirt.

Insights & Observations:

- If your brand is inactive on any of social media channel, it would be advisable not to highlight it on the brand's website. This is becase the people directed to that social media channel may get a very bad impression which can make them not even see the good work that the brand is doing in the other channels.
- Identifying influencers and targeting them to spread word of mouth about the brand would be just one half of the story, better benefits could be obtained if these influencers are given due honors in the community (as Indian Terrain did). This would further motivate not only them but also other community members, and in this manner more influencers could emerge for the brand.
- Directly retweeting the tweet that had brand's mention would not be advisable. By doing so brand looses an opportunity to engage with the community member who tweeted it. In case of long tweets where there are less characters remaining to include additional message, it would be acceptable to retweet, however following it on a regular basis may not yield better results.
- It might not be necessary to create presence on multiple social networking websites for the type of content a brand wishes to be shared with its customers.Sometimes use of appropriate applications can help brand restrict itself to fewer channels and yet achieve richer content delivery.
- Blogs could be used as detailed information resource, especially in product categories where users might face difficulty in evaluating, purchasing and using them. These blogposts could then be shared on other social media channels for better engagement and alternatively driving back the traffic from social media channels to blogs (and hence the website). The traffic could be directed either ways; however the choice remains with the brand and the decision where to have detailed engagement needs has to be made with precision.

10 J. Non-Profit Organizations (Dated:28th January, 2011)

Parameters	*Pratham Books*	*Rang De*	*Deepsikha Cancer Care Foundation*
Social media widgets provided on homepage	Yes	Yes	Yes
Social media presence	Facebook Twitter YouTube Blog Scribd Flickr	Facebook Twitter YouTube Blog	Facebook Twitter YouTube Blog
Facebook			
Welcome Fan tab	No	Yes	No
Info tab details	Yes	Yes	Yes
Integration with other social media tools	No	No	No
Community members can make post/ upload photos, videos	Yes	Yes	Yes
Applications	Events	Experience Newsletter Events	No
Twitter			
Company name	Yes	Yes	Yes
Background image relevant to product	Yes	Yes	No
Location	Bangalore, India	Chennai, India	India
Web address	Corporate Blog	Home website	Home website
Informative bio	Yes	Yes	Yes

YouTube			
About company	Yes	Yes	No
Video themes	Offline events	Offline events	Offline events
Blog			
About blog	Yes	Yes	Yes
Blog post categories	Yes	No	Yes
Archives	Yes	Yes	Yes
Search facility	Yes	No	Yes

There are numerous non-profit organizations in India operating in/for various sectors/causes like education, health, poverty, employment, female rights, cleanliness, etc. Non-profit organizations are in constant need of monetary and manpower support to perform their work effectively and expand their horizon. In India, many non-profit organizations can benefit from co-ordination with others. Social media can aid in spreading word-of-mouth cost effectively and also to gain monetary and/or voluntary support. In this section social media activities undertaken by three non-profit organizations are discussed

PRATHAM BOOKS *(Case Study no. 28)*

Pratham books initiated in 1994, is a non-profit organization which is focused on out-of-school education, and works with the motto of *A Book in Every Child's Hand*[1]. Pratham books published knowledgeable books for children in multiple Indian languages at affordable cost.

Facebook

The Facebook page of Pratham Books used its brand logo as the profile image[2]. Pratham wall posts focused on book promotion, vacancies at the organization, details on offline event in which Pratham Books participated (book fairs, events for kids etc.), details about book launch functions, and achievements by Pratham books, news coverage of Pratham in traditional media, etc. It was noticed that almost every wall post had the link to Pratham's blog. It seemed Pratham's blog was the major information repository and hence the earnest attempt was to make community members to visit their blog regularly. Any kind of information was made available in the form of blog post and the link was shared along with the wall post on the Facebook page. Also, Pratham made extensive use of images, which was evident from the 22 photo albums[3] on its Facebook page. Pratham used the 'Event' application to spread word of mouth about the offline events it organized. The community members too made wallposts on the page expressing their love and satisfaction with the brand, sharing some information resource with the brand etc. Pratham acknowledged these efforts by community members. Though, the ultimate target audience was kids, the pitch was directed to the parents and hence informative content was provided to the parents, so that they could analyze and evaluate the worth of purchasing such products for their kids.

Twitter

The Twitter handle of Pratham Books was @prathambooks[4] and it had a customized Twitter background, something similar to its brand logo. The Bio section detailed the mission of the organization and had reference to its corporate blog in the Web section. Pratham books used Twitter handle for multiple purposes. First, it tweeted about its blogposts, events, achievements, book launches etc. Secondly, it identified news regarding child education, child welfare and retweeted them to its followers. Thirdly and most importantly, maintained engagement with its followers with brand as the focus. When brand's followers made any tweets, Pratham was quick enough to acknowledge them, help them and hence engage them.

YouTube

Pratham Books created its YouTube channel on February 08, 2009[5] and it was named *Pratham Books*. As and when this case study was written the brand had uploaded eight videos. These videos received total upload views of 2,364[6] and had 8 subscribers of this channel. The videos focused on various offline events that Pratham books conducted to build connect with the kids. This channel made a value addition in exhibiting the Pratham's efforts it made in real life, by engaging with the kids (their sought after target segment).

Blog

The Pratham Books blog[7] was well organized and well designed. It had a user interface similar to that of a website, with horizontal tabs (About us, Social Media, Our Offices and Book Reviews) at the top of the page. The right hand margin panel had multiple features – Google Translate application, Facebook page, list of blog post contributors, Twitter updates, search this blog feature, archives, tags and recent comments. Pratham books used its blog as the major interface to disseminate information about the brand to its stakeholders. All information about the brand, product, events, job vacancies at the organization, news about book publishing, achievements etc. was shared through blog posts. One of the main determinants of a book purchase besides it's look and feel is the knowledge of details about the book before a buyer decide to purchase it. Considering the nuances of the product category, Pratham books had an informative content strategy as it tried to share as much information as possible about the product in detail.

Flickr and Scribd

Pratham used Flickr to share images of various offline events it organized and participated in. Further, Pratham used Scribd to share the books that it published. Users could read the entire book from Scribd channel.

RANG DE *(Case Study no. 29)*

Rang De is a Chennai based non-profit organization founded in 2008, deals in peer to peer lending model, helping needy people in their business. It provides microcredit at lower interest rates to under-served. Their long term goal is to build connect between social investors (who can invest their time and money) and the needy people in rural areas. Ramakrishna and Smita co-founded the organization[8] and had Waheeda Rehman and Nagesh Kukunoor as brand ambassadors[9]. As of January 24, 2011, Rang De's efforts had impacted lives of 6,316 borrowers, who were facilitated by 2,445 social investors[10]. The total social investments raised as of January 24, 2011 was Rs. 3,42,78,400 and the social investment repaid was Rs. 1,91,12,247[11]. A social investor could invest any amount in the multiples of Rs.100 in any of the businesses like animal husbandry, bricks business, carpenter, poultry, grocery shop, milk business etc. In case a social investor wasn't interested in choosing a particular beneficiary, he/she could just invest the amount and Rang De would decide to make it available to the best beneficiary. Every borrower returned the amount on a monthly basis along with the interest and the social investor was paid an interest of 2% on his/her investment. Rang De had a sophisticated website, they accepted investments through online transactions and a social investor could easily track the status of the investment made through the website.

Facebook

The Facebook page of Rang De used its brand logo as the profile image[12]. Rang De had a welcome tab, which had a message *Join us to knock out poverty in India[13]*. Rang De made wall posts on various offline events in which Rang De participated, some information about micro-finance industry, blogposts on its blog, video content on micro-finance industry, shared videos from their YouTube channel, updates on the social investments received, etc. Rang De made the posts on it's wall attractive by regular usage of images, videos and weblinks. This would have aided in drawing attention of community members to a large extent. Social investors who regularly made social investments at Rang De were praised by including their names in the wallposts. Events application was utilized to a great extent, as it updated details about all offline events that Rang De organized and participated in. The Newsletter application had a short form to be filled in by community members to receive the same. The content and conversation on this Facebook page was restricted to the cause of eradicating poverty through financing needy people in their businesses.

Twitter

The Twitter handle of Rang De was @RangDe[14] and it had a customized Twitter background with the message *Paint the colours of freedom.* The Bio section detailed Rang De's value proposition. Rang De tweeted about blogposts on its blog, events and news it shared on the Facebook page etc. When Rang De followers tweeted about their investment made in the firm, showed their interest in participating some events organized by Rang De; the brand replied to those tweets acknowledging the efforts made by followers to post such tweets. Rang De also shared some information resources from the micro-finance industry and achievements attained by the brand. The content strategy on Twitter was observed as similar to that of Facebook page.

YouTube

Rang De created its YouTube channel on June 18, 2009[15] and named it as *Rangdeorg*. As and when this case study was written the brand had uploaded 39 videos. These videos received total upload views of 4,230[16] and had 14 subscribers of this channel. The videos focused on various offline events that Rang De participated. There were a couple of videos on their brand ambassador Nagesh Kukunoor and founder Ramakrishna explaining the value proposition offered by Rang De. This channel captured the real life moments of Rang De's participation and reaffirmed its legitimacy, which may be quintessential for a new brand having stepped in with a unique business proposition.

Blog

The Rang De blog was titled as *The Official Rang De Blog*[17]. The blog had a well structured user interface with blog posts aligned on left and details on right margin. The Rang De Facebook page and tweets from their Twitter handle were also featured in the right margin along with the archives. The blog post categories were not created on the blog; hence a user had to browse through the blog posts monthwise from archives section. The earliest blog posts on the blog were traced to August, 2008. Rang De had undertaken blogging activity meticulously and made blog posts on a regular basis, as it was evident from archival section that minimum of 3 blog posts were made in a month to a maximum of 10. The content on blog posts focused on varied topics like achievements of Rang De, details about offline events organized by Rang De, details on Rang De partner meets, contests that were run to promote Rang De, learning's they had from the field, etc.

DEEPSIKHA CANCER CARE FOUNDATION

(Case Study no. 30)

Deepsikha Cancer Care Foundation is a non-profit organization with focus on awareness creation about cancer in North Eastern states of the country[18]. Gradually a strong team of volunteers has been formed in Mumbai, which provides its support to cancer patients. Deepsikha organizes awareness camps, screening camps, stop tobacco centres etc.

Facebook

The Facebook page of Deepsikha Cancer Care Foundation used its brand logo as the profile image[19]. Deepsikha created its Facebook page in November, 2010. It shared information about its offline activities like medical checkup camps, opening of cancer care facilities etc. Deepsikha made use of images in its wall posts to capture the events and share it with community members.

Twitter

The Twitter handle of Deepsikha was @Deepsikhacare and created on December 12, 2010[20]. The bio section had the details about the focus that Deepsikha had in helping cancer patients. As and when this case study was written Deepsikha has made just five tweets. It may be that the content strategy was getting formed and hence the engagement on twitter was not extensive. These tweets were diverse in nature – couple of them redirected the user to its blogposts on topics related to cancer, one tweet redirected to the YouTube channel. Deepsikha started its Twitter journey by following 41[21] Twitter handles, which included various publications that created content related to cancer. So, it could be expected that Deepsikha had plans to share informative content on cancer with its followers in future.

YouTube

Deepsikha created its YouTube channel on November 13, 2010[22] and named it as *DeepsikhaFoundation*. As and when this case study was written the brand had uploaded five videos. These videos received total upload views of 188[23] and had just one subscriber of this channel. The videos were interviews of various spokespersons for the

Deepsikha's efforts. Deepsikha probably had a thought to emphasize its idea through the words of well known spokespersons.

Blog

The Deepsikha blog[24] was initiated in May, 2010. The blog was well organized with well specified blog post categories, archives etc. providing convenient user interface to users. Deepsikha made blog posts on categories like cancer, health and fitness, medical, events, poems etc. The cancer blog posts were focused on topics like chemotherapy, oral health management, risk factors related to oral cancer, breast cancer, prevention and detection of cancer, facts related to cancer etc. The health and fitness category had blog posts focused on role of food in cancer, music therapy for cancer, benefits of running in curing cancer etc. It's clearly evident that such blog posts were intended for spreading awareness about the dreaded disease. The blog also had few blog posts on stories and poems related to cancer.

Insights & Observations:

- Blogs are the one of the best medium to share detailed information with the brand's stakeholders. This information could be related to selection of product, additional information about the product, usage of product, after sales service or could be around a cause as detailed in this chapter. Users generally find it difficult to search and rely on huge information available on Internet. Instead if brands take the initiative of collating the valuable information and sharing the same in a convenient manner, it would be a value addition for the users. However, blogging needs to be done on a continuous basis to maintain the momentum and expectations of the users.
- The content used in blogging should be able to relate to the reader and engage him/her. Further the comments posted by the reader should be attended to well as this can solve the query posted by many other readers at the same point in time.

□

GLOSSARY

A1. Internet Lingo (Abbreviations)

Our explanation of the Social Media will remain incomplete, if we do not leave the readers with the 'short forms' or 'lingo' of conversations in the social media! Let's call them *abbreviations* in context of this glossary. Some of these have which are more commonly used by the Indian *junta*, are expanded and explained below. In some cases we have added some details about the general usage of the abbreviation

2U2: To you too

2day: Today

2morrow: Tomorrow

A/S/L: Age/Sex/Location

AAMOF: As a matter of fact

AFAIK: As Far As I Know

AFK: Away From Keyboard

ASAP: As Soon As Possible

B/W: Between

BF: Boy Friend

BFN: Bye for Now

BRB: Be Right Back -Generally used when you are chatting with someone and you need to take a quick break.

BTW: By the Way

CU: See You

CUL8R: See You Later

CYA: See Ya (You)

DIY: Do It Yourself

EOD: End of Discussion. Used commonly, when there is a chain of conversation going on and someone wants to put an end to that.

Also used when someone wants 'no further discussion'. Also indicates End of Day, when conversations are centred around deadlines.

FAQ: Frequently Asked Questions

FBOW: For Better Or Worse

FOAF: Friend Of A Friend

FYI: For Your Information

GAL: Get a Life – usually used for teasing, but also used sometimes in lighter vein to indicate that there are better things to do in life rather than just carrying on with something frivolous or unimportant.

GF: Girl Friend

GG: Great Game. In the context of the social media used when an online/social multiplayer game ends

GTG: Got to Go

IC: I see

ILU: I Love/Like You

ILY: I Love/Like You

IMAO: In My Arrogant Opinion

IMCO: In My Considered Opinion

IMHO: In My Honest/Humble Opinion

IMNSHO: In My Not So Honest/Humble Opinion

IMO: In My Opinion

IMVHO: In My Very Honest/Humble Opinion

JIC: Just In Case

K: Ok

KISS: Keep It Simple Stupid/Keep It Simple & Straight

KIT: Keep In Touch

L8R: Later

LOL: Laugh Out Loud. Expresses that you are having a hearty laught reading what someone just commented/replied you in chat/ posted as an update etc.

LTNS: Long Time No See

MorF: Male Or Female

N/P: No Problem

NP: No Problem

OMG: Oh My God

PLS: Please

PM: Private Message

ROFL: Rolling on Floor Laughing. Expresses one degree further emotion of Laugh out Loud (LOL) . Exclaims that you just find the comment/status/chat etc too hilarious!

ROTFL: Rolling On The Floor Laughing

SUP: What's Up ?

TANSTAFL: There Ain't No Such Thing As a Free Lunch

TGIF: Thanks God Its Friday

Thx/Txs: Thanks

TIA: Thanks In Advance

TTYL: Talk To You Later

TY/TU: Thank You

W/O: Without

Wt: What?

Whr: Where?

WTG: Way to Go

WU: What's Up

WYSIWYG: What You See Is What You Get

Y?: Why?

ZZZ: Sleeping. This is used to indicate that you are getting bored with the conversation or if you are too tired etc. Whatever may be the context of the usage, you want to convey, that you feel like sleeping!

There is also a list of abbreviations which contain language used **unparliamentarily.** We have elaborated some of these to the extent possible and used '*' in place of letters, where deemed appropriate.

KMA: Kiss My A**

LMAO: Laughing My A** Off

ROFLMAO: Rolling On Floor Laughing My A** Off

ROTFLMAO: Rolling On The Floor Laughing My A** Off

WTF: What the F***

A2. Terminology

Some of the commonly used terms in the context of Social Media are outlined in the section .below. This may help in engaging in an 'intelligent' communication or conversation on a twitter account a Facebook page or a blog.

Aggregation: There are multiple websites which publish content on the same topic. For e.g. news channels covering the same story, critics writing review of the same movie etc. Aggregators may be a website or a software which 'aggregates' the information sought (by the user) on a specific topic (movie, news etc). Eg: Google Reader

Alerts: If you specify a tag, a phrase or a word which may be related to a broad topic like "India" to a very specific topic like " FIFA World Cup" , the search engines like Google, send an email to your account updating on the the most recent information on this particular topic that you select. These email update is referred to as an Alert[1]

Applications: Application is technically known as application software and also simply known as *app.* It is computer software which could be designed for a specific task. Brands create such applications and use them along with their Facebook page to engage with customers. These applications could be purely utility based or for entertainment purpose.

Archive: Preserving (collecting) the data at one place (archive site) is referred to as archiving. One such example is Google News. When you search for news and it's not current, you can find it out in "Archives'. Similarly in Blogs, the articles are referenced month/ week/year wise as "Archives'.

Asynchronous communications: In this mode of communication, sender and receiver of a message aren't present in real time (as that of mobile). Sender sends a message at a particular time instant and receiver would read it after some time lag.

Avatars: It is an image or a 3- D model, which is a graphical representation of the user. In some of the games/portals you can choose, clothing, behavior, hair style, body type etc.

Blogs *(noun)*: A website where a user or an organization (corporate or otherwise) posts (known as 'blogs ' (*verb*)) content in the form of text, image or a video. The readers of this can usually post their comments on the content they like and the content they don't. Each 'post' may have 'tags' (see details in "Tags" below) which can be used to identify the content. All the content posted in blog is usually stored chronologically as '*archives*'

Blogroll: In the sidebar list, this is the list which may contain 'hyperlinks' to the blogs that a blogger often/regularly reads and/or may recommend to his/her readers

Community: An Online community comprises of a group of people coming together for a liking , a cause, an area of interest or anything else which they share in common. These are commonly formed in social networking websites like Facebook, Linkedin etc .In facebook, the members of the community can post comments on the "Wall" of the community –similarly in other SNSs there are different modes of communication for the members There is a moderator for the community who monitors the content posted. Some communities are also formed by corporate for promoting their products/services.

Community Manager: Every brand/organization etc usually appoints an individual to manage it's tFacebook page, Twitter handle, who is commonly referred to as community manager. The community manager is the touch point for community members of the brand. The community manager holds the responsibility of planning, scheduling and posting content, responding to comments, queries etc. Sometimes a brand might have multiple community managers in order to ensure spontaneous response and to share the workload.

Community Members: The group of people who "like" a Facebook page or "follow" a Twitter handle are referred to as community The community could consist of current customers, prospective customers, suppliers, competitors etc., -in short any stakeholder.

Crowdsourcing: The process of getting a typical task done by a larger group of people or the *crowd* who do not belong to the organization. This task which was earlier done in-house, like asking for suggestions to solve a business issue or seeking inputs for product conceptualization etc. Throwing open the problem to a large group of people may benefit the faster resolution and sometimes an out of the box solution.

Facebook page: Page that can be created on Facebook for "organizations, businesses, celebrities, and bands"[2] . These can be utilized for broadcasting information in an official, public[3] manner with those who connect with this Facebook page.

Folksonomy: This term is a coined by Thomas Vander Wal[3]. Folksonomy is generated when people tag any content with URL for their own retrieval later[4]. This is done in an environment which is social and shared to others usually[5]. Such an activity of tagging is also known as "Social Classification" and can be seen at Flickr where people tag photos and the most popular of these tags float on the top[6].Please note that there are other such classification being done for all other forms of content like videos, text etc too in other social channels.

Hashtags: Whenever you add a "#" (Hashtag symbol) in any word that you write as a tweet , it gets marked. If anyone searches for a tweet with the 'word' that you had incorporated in your tweet by using '#word', then your tweet shows up easily. Thus hashtags, categorizes[14] tweets. On clicking the word with a hashtag, all tweets which have a similar categorization show up.

Mashups: When a new and innovative[18] service gets created by a web application usually interactive, by bringing together content from two or more sources, it's known as a Mashup.

Pagerank: When a keyword search is made in a search engine, the search engine displays results. The position of a particular content in the search result is known as pagerank. For e.g. if a particular blog appears 3rd in the search results, the pagerank of that blog could be called as 3. The higher the pagerank, better the probability of content being read by the user.

Permalink: URL pointing to a specific entry either in a blog[7] or forum once it is archived

Photoblog: A blog where the content is primarily photos.

Podcast: This word was coined in 2004 by Ben Hammersley[8]. It refers to an audio or video file(s) that can be accessed by you for listening and/or watching[9]. The general usage of the word is for referring to a series of such files (it's general usage).

Vlog: is a video blog, where the content is primarily in the form of videos.

Vlogger: a person who maintains a Vlog is known as a Video Blogger or aVlogger

ReTweet: When a user finds a particular tweet very interesting, he/she might think that this tweet would be valuable for his/her followers, it could be just shared with them without adding any remarks/ views to it. It is often referred to as "RT"[20].

RSS (Really Simple Syndication): If you would like to be regularly updated with the new content on a blog or a websites or to aggregate the same updates from many website, an RSS *feed* enables you to do it. Nowadays almost all blogs and numerous sites have an RSS enablement, where you can subscribe to the updates by just clicking on an icon. These feeds can be read using **RSS Aggregator**, RSS Reader[18].

RSVP: It is a French word, which simply means expressing one's wish to attend an event to which he/she has been invited[21]. In Facebook, when an event is posted and shared with the community members, they could share their intention of attending that event by clicking on either of three options – Yes, No, May be Attending. This data helps the organizers to arrange for required logistics.

SEO: SEO is an acronym of Search Engine Optimization, which is a technical aspect of Internet marketing[22]. It involves optimizing web pages of a particular website or the entire website in a manner they become search-friendly, and they appear higher in the search results (higher pagerank). Basically, it involves including relevant content on the webpages and use of certain keywords that search engines could track when users use those keywords to search information for their requirement.

Social Media Dashboard: It is a tool which could be used to monitor brand's activities across many social media channels. It simplifies the task of managing multiple social media channels from one place. There are many social media dashboards available in the industry, some of the popular ones are Hootsuite, Seesmic, CoTweet, Tweetdeck etc.[23] These dashboards could be downloaded on the laptop/ computer, and the user then needs to add all social media channels to this dashboard.

Tags: They are the keywords that are related to the extended content. When information seekers search for content, they generally use keywords, which help them reaching the sought after content.

Tweet: The short message that a user shares with followers is called *tweet* in the context of Twitter. A tweet has the maximum limit of 140 characters.

Twitter Handle: The username selected by you and the URL[13] (www.twitter.com/username) is referred to as the twitter handle. It has been observed that when asked about their twitter handles, people usually responsd with "@username" . For example if a person has selected a user name Kabir786 , then he/she will usually share the twitter handle as @Kabir786 when asked for it.

Virtual Worlds: This term describes a simulated environment on the internet which is interactive and is accessed by users (multiple).

VOIP: this is a term used to refer to a set of facilities[11] (technologies, protocols etc) which enable voice communication over the internet.

Wall post: A message shared by an user on his/her wall is called as wall post. This message could be purely in text form, or a user could attach a photo/video/weblink along with the text message to provide enriched information to his/her network friends. The maximum characters of a wall post on Facebook are 420 characters[24].

Web 2.0: in very simple words a website or a web application can be referred to as a 'Web 2.0' website or application if it allows interaction and collaboration[15] between the users. While Web 1.0 has often been referred to as a 'static' web, Web 2.0 on a broad basis refers to 'interactive'[16] web. Web 2.0 websites are usually with an attractive and preferably a *light* graphical user interface.

Widget: It can be termed as a small application or a program[19] that can be put on a website or a blog Eg: A small clock, calendar, image viewer etc.

Wiki: This is a collaborative website where users can either create or edit a page. There are various levels of access in each wiki. While in a public wiki, users may be able to edit content even without logging in, in a private wiki the users are required to log in. The record of the previous version is kept by most of the wikis. [10]

□

REFERENCES

Chap 1: Introduction

1. Zuckerbeg,M.,'500Million Stories', http://blog.facebook.com/blog.php?post=409753352130&ref=mf, July21, 2010 (Last accessed on 26th January, 2011)
2. Grossman, L., 'Mark Zuckerberg', http://www.time.com/time/specials/packages/article/0,28804,2036683_2037183_2037185,00.html, December 15, 2010 (Last accessed on 26th January 2011)
3. Rosenberg, J., 'TIME's Man of the Year List', http://history1900s.about.com/od/people/a/Man-Of-The-Year.htm (Last accessed on 26th January 2011)
4. 'About Twitter', http://twitter.com/about (Last accessed on 29th January 2011)

Chapter 2: What is Social Media?

1. 'Networking: Weak ties, strong ties, and their implications', http://www.techiteasy.org/2008/08/23/networking-weak-ties-strong-ties-and-their-implications/(Last accessed on 2nd February, 2011)
2. 'Facebook Factsheet', http://www.facebook.com/press/info.php?factsheet (Last accessed on 3rd February, 2011)
3. 'Facebook Factsheet', http://www.facebook.com/press/info.php?factsheet (Last accessed on 3rd February, 2011)
4. 'All Apps', http://www.facebook.com/apps/directory.php (Last accessed on 3rd February, 2011)
5. 'Facebook Pages', http://www.facebook.com/help/?page=175 (Last accessed on 3rd February, 2011)
6. 'Facebook Groups', http://www.facebook.com/groups/(Last accessed on 3rd February, 2011)
7. 'Twitter', http://en.wikipedia.org/wiki/Twitter (Last accessed on 3rd February, 2011)
8. 'About Twitter', http://twitter.com/about (Last accessed on 3rd February, 2011)

9. 'About Us', http://press.linkedin.com/about/(Last accessed on 3rd February, 2011)
10. 'Answers', http://learn.linkedin.com/answers/(Last accessed on 3rd February, 2011)
11. 'Groups', http://learn.linkedin.com/groups/(Last accessed on 3rd February, 2011)
12. 'LinkedIn Jobs', http://learn.linkedin.com/jobs/overview2/(Last accessed on 3rd February, 2011)
13. 'Company Pages', http://learn.linkedin.com/company-pages/(Last accessed on 3rd February, 2011)
14. 'Timeline', http://www.youtube.com/t/press_timeline (Last accessed on 3rd February, 2011)
15. 'What is Slideshare?', http://www.slideshare.net/about (Last accessed on 3rd February, 2011)

Chapter 3: Demystifying Twitter

1. 'Following Rules and Best Practices', http://support.twitter.com/articles/68916-following-rules-and-best-practices, (Last accessed on 1st February, 2011)

Chapter 5: How lives are changing on a personal basis

1. 'Maslow's Hierarchy of Needs', http://en.wikipedia.org/wiki/Maslow%27s_hierarchy_of_needs (Last accessed on 29th Jan 2011)
2. 'Twenty20', http://en.wikipedia.org/wiki/Twenty20 (Last accessed on 29th Jan 2011)
3. http://www.iplt20.com/(Last accessed on 29th Jan 2011)
4. 'IPL has Eclipsed TRP of Hindi Entertainment Channels', March 4, 2010, http://www.iplpulse.com/columns/ipl-has-eclipsed-gec-of-hindi-entertainment-channels/(Last accessed on 29th Jan 2011)
5. Foley, S. , 'How Yum! Brands is Conquering the World', July 14, 2010, http://www.businessweek.com/globalbiz/content/jul2010/gb20100714_088544.htm (Last accessed on 29th Jan 2011)
6. http://censusindia.gov.in/Census_And_You/age_structure_and_marital_status.aspx (Last accessed on 29th Jan 2011)
7. 'Asia', http://www.internetworldstats.com/asia.htm (Last accessed on 29th Jan 2011)

Chapter 6: How should firms frame social media strategy?

1. Owyang, J., 'Report: Companies should Organize for Social Media in a 'Hub and Spoke' Model', http://www.web-strategist.com/blog/2009/06/25/report-companies-should-organize-for-social-media-in-hub-

and-spoke/, June 25, 2009 (Last accessed on 1st February, 2011)

2. '13 Most Popular Professional Networking Sites', http://www.veristlabs.com/resources/13-most-popular-professional-networking-sites.html, August 12, 2010 (Last accessed on 1st February, 2011)
3. '10 Popular Social Networking Sites Geographic Wise', http://www.articlesbase.com/internet-marketing-articles/10-popular-social-networking-sites-geographic-wise-3332003.html, September 24, 2010 (Last accessed on 1st February, 2011)
4. YinGuang, J., 'Qq.com China's Most Popular Portal in December: ACNielsen', http://www.thechinaperspective.com/articles/qqcomchina039smostpopularportalindecemberacnielsen6922/index.html, February 08, 2010 (Last accessed on 1st February, 2011)

Chapter 8: Social media utility beyond business

1. 'Use of Social Network Websites in Investigations', http://en.wikipedia.org/wiki/Use_of_social_network_websites_in_investigations (Last accessed on 30th January 2011)
2. 'Crowdsourcing', http://en.wikipedia.org/wiki/Crowdsourcing (Last accessed on 31st January 2011)
3. 'What is Yahoo Answers?', August 04, 2010, http://help.yahoo.com/l/us/yahoo/answers/overview/overview-55778.html (Last accessed on 31st January 2011)
4. 'Help Center', http://www.facebook.com/help/?page=828 (Last accessed on 31st January 2011)

Chapter 9: Social Media Influence & Opportunities

1. Jahns, R. G. and Mikalajunaite, E. (2010), 'The Smartphone Application Market has reached more than 2.2 Billion Dollars in the First Half of 2010', http://www.research2guidance.com/the-smartphone-application-market-has-reached-more-than-2.2-billion-dollars-in-the-first-half-of-2010/, August, 19, 2010 (Last accessed on 31st January 2011)
2. 'What is AdSense', http://www.google.com/support/adsense/bin/static.py?hl=en&page=guide.cs&guide=29574&from=29574&rd=2 (Last accessed on 31st January 2011)
3. 'How much will I Earn with AdSense?', http://www.google.com/support/adsense/bin/answer.py?hl=en&answer=9902 (Last accessed on 31st January 2011)
4. 'Social Casual Games', http://en.wikipedia.org/wiki/Social_casual_games (Last accessed on 31st January 2011)

5. http://www.zynga.com/about/index.php (Last accessed on 31st January 2011)
6. 'Social Gaming Market to Surpass $1 billion', http://www.emarketer.com/Article.aspx?R=1008166, January 12, 2011 (Last accessed on 31st January 2011)
7. Trefis Team, 'Is Facebook Flipping Off Mickey, Rupert and Sumner?', http://blogs.forbes.com/greatspeculations/2011/01/28/is-facebook-flipping-off-mickey-rupert-and-sumner/, January 28, 2011(Last accessed on 31st January 2011)

Chapter 10 A. Telecom Service Providers

1. 'Airtel Unveils New Youthful and Dynamic Global Identity', http://www.airtel.in/wps/wcm/connect/About%20Bharti%20Airtel/bharti+airtel/media+centre/bharti+airtel+news/corporate/pg-airtel_unveils_new_youthful_and_dynamic_global_identity (Last accessed on 20th December, 2010)
2. http://www.facebook.com/help/?page=900#!/AirtelIN (Last accessed on 20th December, 2010)
3. The status update was posted on the wall on January 12, 2011 at 5:52pm, http://www.facebook.com/Airtel_IN#!/AirtelIN?v=wall (Last accessed on 20th December, 2010)
4. http://www.facebook.com/help/?page=900#!/AirtelIN?v=app_4949752878 (Last accessed on 20th December, 2010)
5. http://twitter.com/airtel_in (Last accessed on 20th December, 2010)
6. http://twitter.com/airtel_in (Last accessed on 20th December, 2010)
7. http://twitter.com/airtel_presence (Last accessed on 20th December, 2010)
8. http://www.youtube.com/user/INAirtel (Last accessed on 20th December, 2010)
9. http://www.youtube.com/user/INAirtel#g/a (Last accessed on 20th December, 2010)
10. http://www.facebook.com/help/?page=900#!/vodafoneessar (Last accessed on 20th December, 2010)
11. http://www.facebook.com/vodafoneessar?v=app_10531514314 (Last accessed on 20th December, 2010)
12. http://www.facebook.com/vodafoneessar?v=app_10531514314#!/vodafoneessar?v=app_7146470109 (Last accessed on 20th December, 2010)
13. http://www.facebook.com/vodafoneessar?v=app_10531514314#!/vodafoneessar?v=app_4949752878 (Last accessed on 20th December, 2010)

14. http://www.facebook.com/vodafoneessar?v=app_10531514314#!/vodafoneessar?v=app_2373072738 (Last accessed on 20th December, 2010)
15. http://twitter.com/vodafoneIN (Last accessed on 20th December, 2010)
16. http://www.facebook.com/idea (Last accessed on 20th December, 2010)
17. http://www.facebook.com/idea#!/idea?v=app_4949752878 (Last accessed on 20th December, 2010)
18. http://twitter.com/ideacellular (Last accessed on 20th December, 2010)
19. http://www.youtube.com/user/ideacellularltd (Last accessed on 20th December, 2010)
20. http://www.youtube.com/user/ideacellularltd#g/a (Last accessed on 20th December, 2010)

Chapter 10 B. Book Retailing

1. www.flipkart.com
2. http://www.facebook.com/flipkart?v=wall (Last accessed on 20th December, 2010)
3. http://www.facebook.com/flipkart?v=app_6261817190 (Last accessed on 20th December, 2010)
4. http://twitter.com/flipkart (Last accessed on 20th December, 2010)
5. Figures as of 20th December, 2010
6. http://blog.flipkart.com/(Last accessed on 20th December, 2010)
7. http://dialabook.in/about/(Last accessed on 20th December, 2010)
8. http://www.facebook.com/dialabook (Last accessed on 20th December, 2010)
9. http://twitter.com/dialabook (Last accessed on 20th December, 2010)
10. Figures as of 20th December, 2010

Chapter 10 C. Accessories

1. http://www.fastrack.in/About_Fastrack/About_Us.aspx (Last accessed on 26th December, 2010)
2. http://www.facebook.com/pages/Fastrack/22353108376 (Last accessed on 26th December, 2010)
3. http://www.facebook.com/pages/Fastrack/22353108376#!/album.php?aid=235649&id=22353108376 (Last accessed on 26th December, 2010)
4. http://www.facebook.com/pages/Fastrack/22353108376#!/pages/Fastrack/22353108376?v=app_10467688569 (Last accessed on 26th December, 2010)
5. http://www.facebook.com/pages/Fastrack/2
Fastrack/22353108376?v=app_103394

December, 2010)

6. http://www.facebook.com/pages/Fastrack/22353108376#!/pages/Fastrack/22353108376?v=app_83338428339 (Last accessed on 26th December, 2010)
7. http://www.facebook.com/pages/Fastrack/22353108376#!/pages/Fastrack/22353108376?v=app_112321628778648 (Last accessed on 26th December, 2010)
8. http://twitter.com/fastrack (Last accessed on 26th December, 2010)
9. http://www.youtube.com/user/fastrackworld (Last accessed on 26th December, 2010)
10. http://www.youtube.com/user/fastrackworld#g/a (Last accessed on 26th December, 2010)
11. www.wildcraft.in (Last accessed on 26th December, 2010)
12. http://www.facebook.com/pages/Fastrack/22353108376#!/wildcraft?v=app_10531514314 (Last accessed on 26th December, 2010)
13. http://twitter.com/wildcraftnews (Last accessed on 26th December, 2010)
14. Figures as of 26th December, 2010

Chapter 10 D. Automobiles

1. http://www.facebook.com/MahindraScorpio (Last accessed on 30th December, 2010)
2. http://www.facebook.com/home.php#!/MahindraScorpio?v=app_242981388576 (Last accessed on 30th December, 2010)
3. http://www.facebook.com/home.php#!/MahindraScorpio?v=photos (Last accessed on 30th December, 2010)
4. https://twitter.com/mahindrascorpio (Last accessed on 30th December, 2010)
5. Figures as of 30th December, 2010
6. http://www.youtube.com/user/scorpioadmin#p/a (Last accessed on 30th December, 2010)
7. http://www.youtube.com/user/scorpioadmin#g/a (Last accessed on 30th December, 2010)
8. http://www.flickr.com/photos/mahindrascorpio (Last accessed on 30th December, 2010)
9. http://www.flickr.com/photos/mahindrascorpio/archives/(Last accessed on 30th December, 2010)
10. http://www.facebook.com/marutisuzukisx4 (Last accessed on 30th December, 2010)
11. http://www.facebook.com/marutisuzukisx4#!/marutisuzukisx4?v=app_125467654178992 (Last accessed on 30th December, 2010)
12. http://www.facebook.com/marutisuzukisx4#!/marutisuzukisx4?v=app_

4949752878 (Last accessed on 30th December, 2010)

13. http://www.facebook.com/marutisuzukisx4#!/marutisuzukisx4?v=photos (Last accessed on 30th December, 2010)
14. Post was made on 11th December, 2010 at 6.43 pm
15. http://twitter.com/marutisuzukisx4 (Last accessed on 30th December, 2010)
16. Figures as of December 30, 2010 (Last accessed on 30th December, 2010)
17. http://www.youtube.com/marutisuzukisx4 (Last accessed on 30th December, 2010)
18. http://www.youtube.com/marutisuzukisx4#g/c/688F56D879D750EF (Last accessed on 30th December, 2010)
19. http://www.flickr.com/photos/marutisx4 (Last accessed on 30th December, 2010)
20. http://www.flickr.com/photos/marutisx4/archives/(Last accessed on 30th December, 2010)
21. http://www.facebook.com/TataNanoPage (Last accessed on 30th December, 2010)
22. http://twitter.com/tatanano_tweets (Last accessed on 30th December, 2010)
23. Figures as of 30th December, 2010

Chapter 10 E. FMCG

1. http://www.facebook.com/chingssecret?v=app_4949752878 (Last accessed on 2nd January, 2011)
2. http://twitter.com/chingssecret (Last accessed on 2nd January, 2011)
3. Figures as of 2nd January, 2011
4. http://www.youtube.com/user/chingssecret (Last accessed on 2nd January, 2011)
5. http://www.youtube.com/user/chingssecret#g/a (Last accessed on 2nd January, 2011)
6. http://www.facebook.com/pages/HIPPO-/173604292745 (Last accessed on 2nd January, 2011)
7. http://twitter.com/HelloMeHippo (Last accessed on 2nd January, 2011)
8. http://twitter.com/HelloMeHippo (Last accessed on 2nd January, 2011)
9. Figures as of 2nd January, 2011
10. http://www.facebook.com/waghbakri (Last accessed on 2nd January, 2011)
11. http://twitter.com/waghbakri (Last accessed on 2nd January, 2011)
12. Figures as of 2nd January, 2011
13. http://www.facebook.com/Kurkure (Last accessed on 2nd January, 2011)

14. http://www.facebook.com/Kurkure?v=photos (Last accessed on 2nd January, 2011)
15. http://www.youtube.com/user/kurkure (Last accessed on 2nd January, 2011)
16. http://www.youtube.com/user/kurkure#g/u (Last accessed on 2nd January, 2011)
17. http://www.facebook.com/happydentgum (Last accessed on 2nd January, 2011)
18. http://www.facebook.com/happydentgum?v=photos (Last accessed on 2nd January, 2011)

Chapter 10 F. Insurance

1. http://www.facebook.com/licindia?v=wall (Last accessed on 22nd January, 2011)
2. http://www.facebook.com/LICIndiaForever (Last accessed on 22nd January, 2011)
3. http://www.facebook.com/LICIndiaForever (Last accessed on 22nd January, 2011)
4. http://www.facebook.com/LICIndiaForever?v=info (Last accessed on 22nd January, 2011).
5. http://www.facebook.com/LICIndiaForever?v=app_7146470109 (Last accessed on 22nd January, 2011)
6. http://twitter.com/licindiaforever (Last accessed on 22nd January, 2011)
7. http://www.youtube.com/user/LICIndiaForever?blend=1&ob=5 (Last accessed on 22nd January, 2011)
8. http://www.facebook.com/HDFClife (Last accessed on 22nd January, 2011)
9. http://www.facebook.com/pages/HDFC-STANDARD-LIFE-INSURANCE/243666169331?v=wall (Last accessed on 22nd January, 2011)
10. http://www.facebook.com/pages/HDFC-STANDARD-LIFE-INSURANCE/243666169331 (Last accessed on 22nd January, 2011)
11. http://twitter.com/hdfclife (Last accessed on 22nd January, 2011)
12. http://twitter.com/hdfclife (Last accessed on 22nd January, 2011)
13. http://www.linkedin.com/company/hdfc-standard-life-insurance (Last accessed on 22nd January, 2011)
14. Data retrieved as of 22nd January, 2011 from LinkedIn page
15. http://learn.linkedin.com/company-pages/(Last accessed on 22nd January, 2011)
16. http://www.facebook.com/jiyobefikar?v=wall (Last accessed on 22nd January, 2011)

17. http://www.facebook.com/jiyobefikar?v=app_4949752878 (Last accessed on 22nd January, 2011)
18. http://twitter.com/jiyobefikar (Last accessed on 22nd January, 2011)
19. http://twitter.com/jiyobefikar (Last accessed on 22nd January, 2011)
20. http://twitter.com/jiyobefikar (Last accessed on 22nd January, 2011)
21. http://www.youtube.com/user/jiyobefikar?blend=1&ob=5 (Last accessed on 22nd January, 2011)
22. http://www.youtube.com/user/jiyobefikar?blend=1&ob=5#g/u (Last accessed on 22nd January, 2011)

Chapter 10 G. Airlines

1. http://www.facebook.com/jetairways?v=wall (Last accessed on 24th January, 2011)
2. http://www.facebook.com/jetairways?v=photos (Last accessed on 24th January, 2011)
3. http://twitter.com/jetairways (Last accessed on 24th January, 2011)
4. http://www.youtube.com/jetairways#g/a (Last accessed on 24th January, 2011)
5. http://www.youtube.com/jetairways#g/a (Last accessed on 24th January, 2011)
6. http://www.flickr.com/photos/jetairways (Last accessed on 24th January, 2011)
7. http://www.flickr.com/photos/jetairways/archives/date-taken/2011/01/10/(Last accessed on 24th January, 2011)
8. http://www.facebook.com/FlyKingfisher?ref=ts#!/FlyKingfisher?v=wall (Last accessed on 24th January, 2011)
9. www.youtube.com/KingofGoodtimes (Last accessed on 24th January, 2011)
10. www.kingfisherholidays.com
11. http://twitter.com/flykingfisher (Last accessed on 24th January, 2011)
12. http://www.facebook.com/pages/SpiceJet/188319247533?v=wall (Last accessed on 24th January, 2011)
13. http://twitter.com/flyspicejet (Last accessed on 24th January, 2011)
14. Information from bio section of Twitter handle @flyspicejet
15. http://www.youtube.com/user/flyspicejet#g/u (Last accessed on 24th January, 2011)
16. http://www.youtube.com/user/flyspicejet#g/u (Last accessed on 24th January. 2011)
17. http://www.youtube.com/user/flyspicejet#g/a (Last accessed on 24th January, 2011)

Chapter 10 H. Multiplexes

1. http://www.facebook.com/pages/PVR-Cinemas/143035365719744?v=info (Last accessed on 25th January, 2011)
2. http://www.facebook.com/pages/PVR-Cinemas/143035365719744?v=photos (Last accessed on 25th January, 2011)
3. http://apps.facebook.com/pvrcinemas/?ref=ts (Last accessed on 25th January, 2011)
4. http://twitter.com/_pvrcinemas (Last accessed on 25th January, 2011)
5. http://twitter.com/_pvrcinemas (Last accessed on 25th January, 2011)
6. http://www.youtube.com/user/pvrchannel (Last accessed on 25th January, 2011)
7. http://www.youtube.com/user/pvrchannel#g/a (Last accessed on 25th January, 2011)
8. http://www.facebook.com/BigCinemasIndia?ref=ts (Last accessed on 25th January, 2011)
9. http://www.facebook.com/BigCinemasIndia?v=app_6261817190 (Last accessed on 25th January, 2011)
10. http://www.facebook.com/BigCinemasIndia?v=app_110992342299752 (Last accessed on 25th January, 2011)
11. http://www.facebook.com/BigCinemasIndia?v=photos (Last accessed on 25th January, 2011)
12. http://www.youtube.com/user/RelianceBigCinemas (Last accessed on 25th January, 2011)
13. http://www.youtube.com/user/RelianceBigCinemas#g/a (Last accessed on 25th January, 2011)
14. http://www.youtube.com/profile?user=RelianceBigCinemas&view=subscriptions (Last accessed on 25th January, 2011)
15. http://www.facebook.com/pages/INOX-Leisure-Ltd/145266579078?v=wall (Last accessed on 25th January, 2011)
16. http://twitter.com/inoxleisure (Last accessed on 25th January, 2011)

Chapter 10 I. Apparels

1. http://www.facebook.com/indianterrain?v=wall (Last accessed on 27th January, 2011)
2. http://www.facebook.com/indianterrain?v=info (Last accessed on 27th January, 2011)
3. Wall post made on 24th January, 2011, 5.25 pm. http://www.facebook.com/indianterrain?v=wall (Last accessed on 27th January, 2011)
4. Wall post made on 12th December, 2010, 4.39 pm http://www.facebook.com/indianterrain?v=wall (Last accessed on 27th January, 2011)

5. Wall post made on 24th November, 2010, 3.43 pm http://www.facebook.com/indianterrain?v=wall (Last accessed on 27th January, 2011)
6. http://www.facebook.com/indianterrain?v=app_10531514314 (Last accessed on 27th January, 2011)
7. http://www.youtube.com/changewithIT (Last accessed on 27th January, 2011)
8. http://www.youtube.com/changewithIT (Last accessed on 27th January, 2011)
9. http://www.facebook.com/pantaloons (Last accessed on 27th January, 2011)
10. http://www.facebook.com/pantaloons?v=photos (Last accessed on 27th January, 2011)
11. http://twitter.com/pantaloonsindia (Last accessed on 27th January, 2011)
12. http://twitter.com/pantaloonsindia (Last accessed on 27th January, 2011)
13. Twitpic is an application that helped users to upload image along with their tweets, www.twitpic.com. It was a free service.
14. http://www.youtube.com/user/PantaloonsFashion (Last accessed on 27th January, 2011)
15. http://www.youtube.com/user/PantaloonsFashion#p/u/0/X1kTGzHMG-4 (Last accessed on 27th January, 2011)
16. http://www.youtube.com/user/PantaloonsFashion#g/a (Last accessed on 27th January, 2011)
17. www.teesort.com
18. http://www.teesort.com/online-t-shirt-company.htm (Last accessed on 27th January, 2011)
19. http://www.facebook.com/teesort?v=wall (Last accessed on 27th January, 2011)
20. http://www.facebook.com/teesort?v=app_153559371347196 (Last accessed on 27th January, 2011)
21. http://www.facebook.com/teesort?v=app_100265896690345 (Last accessed on 27th January, 2011)
22. http://www.facebook.com/teesort?v=app_123675280994484 (Last accessed on 27th January, 2011)
23. http://www.facebook.com/teesort?v=app_133498836675632 (Last accessed on 27th January, 2011)
24. http://twitter.com/teesort (Last accessed on 27th January, 2011)
25. http://www.teesort.com/blog/(Last accessed on 27th January, 2011)
26. http://www.teesort.com/blog/category/about-teesort (Last accessed on 27th January, 2011)
27. http://www.teesort.com/blog/category/cricket-mania (Last accessed on 27th January, 2011)

28. http://www.teesort.com/blog/category/fashionista (Last accessed on 27th January, 2011)

Chapter 10 J. Non-Profit Organizations

1. www.prathambooks.org
2. http://www.facebook.com/prathambooks (Last accessed on 28th January, 2011)
3. http://www.facebook.com/prathambooks?v=photos (Last accessed on 28th January, 2011)
4. http://twitter.com/prathambooks (Last accessed on 28th January, 2011)
5. http://www.youtube.com/user/prathambooks (Last accessed on 28th January, 2011)
6. http://www.youtube.com/user/prathambooks#g/a (Last accessed on 28th January, 2011)
7. http://blog.prathambooks.org/(Last accessed on 28th January, 2011)
8. http://www.rangde.org/team.htm (Last accessed on 28th January, 2011)
9. http://www.rangde.org/ambassador.htm (Last accessed on 28th January, 2011)
10. www.rangde.org (Last accessed on 28th January, 2011)
11. www.rangde.org (Last accessed on 28th January, 2011)
12. http://www.facebook.com/rangdeorg?v=wall (Last accessed on 28th January, 2011)
13. http://www.facebook.com/rangdeorg?v=app_103199439735866 (Last accessed on 28th January, 2011)
14. http://twitter.com/rangde (Last accessed on 28th January, 2011)
15. http://www.youtube.com/rangdeorg (Last accessed on 28th January, 2011)
16. http://www.youtube.com/rangdeorg#g/a (Last accessed on 28th January, 2011)
17. http://blog.rangde.org/(Last accessed on 28th January, 2011)
18. www.deepsikha.org
19. http://www.facebook.com/pages/Deepsikha-Cancer-Care-Foundation/109578379107874 (Last accessed on 28th January, 2011)
20. http://twitter.com/deepsikhacare (Last accessed on 28th January, 2011)
21. http://twitter.com/deepsikhacare/following (Last accessed of 28th January, 2011)
22. http://www.youtube.com/user/deepsikhafoundation (Last accessed on 28th January, 2011)
23. http://www.youtube.com/user/deepsikhafoundation#g/a (Last accessed on 28th January, 2011)
24. http://blog.deepsikha.org (Last accessed on 28th January, 2011)

Glossary-A2: Terminology

1. http://www.google.com/alerts (Last accessed on 22nd January, 2011)
2. 'Help Center', http://www.facebook.com/help/?page=904 (Last accessed on 23rd January, 2011)
3. Vander Wal, T. 'Folksonomy', February2, 2007, http://vanderwal.net/folksonomy.html (Last accessed on 23rd January, 2011)
4. do
5. do
6. Smith, G. 'Folksonomy: Social Classification', August 3, 2004, http://atomiq.org/archives/2004/08/folksonomy_social_classification.html (Last accessed on 23rd January, 2011)
7. 'Permalink', http://en.wikipedia.org/wiki/Permalink (Last accessed on 25th January, 2011)
8. Hammersley, B. 'Audible Revolution', Ferbuary 12, 2004, http://www.guardian.co.uk/media/2004/feb/12/broadcasting.digitalmedia (Last accessed on 26th January, 2011)
9. 'What is a Podcast?', http://blog.podcast.com/podcastcom-faq/what-is-a-podcast/(Last accessed on 26th January, 2011)
10. 'Wiki', http://en.wikipedia.org/wiki/Wiki (Last accessed on 26th January, 2011)
11. 'VoIP', http://searchunifiedcommunications.techtarget.com/definition/VoIP (Last accessed on 26th January, 2011)
12. 'What is a Virtual World?', http://www.virtualworldsreview.com/info/whatis.shtml (Last accessed on 26th January, 2011)
13. 'The Twitter Glossary', http://support.twitter.com/groups/31-twitter-basics/topics/104-welcome-to-twitter-support/articles/166337-the-twitter-glossary#h (Last accessed on 26th January, 2011)
14. 'What are Hashtags ('#' Symbols)?', http://support.twitter.com/articles/49309-what-are-hashtags-symbols (Last accessed on 26th January, 2011)
15. O'Reilly, T. 'What is Web 2.0', http://oreilly.com/pub/a/web2/archive/what-is-web-20.html?page=5 (Last accessed on 26th January, 2011)
16. 'Web 2.0', http://en.wikipedia.org/wiki/Web_2.0 (Last accessed on 26th January, 2011)
17. 'RSS', http://en.wikipedia.org/wiki/RSS (Last accessed on 26th January, 2011)
18. Merrill, D., 'Mashups: The New Breed of Web App', http://www.ibm.com/developerworks/xml/library/x-mashups.html (Last accessed on 26th January, 2011)
19. Nations, D., 'What are Web Widgets', http://webtrends.about.com/od/widgets/a/what_is_widget.htm (Last accessed on 26th January, 2011)
20. 'What is Retweet? (RT)', http://support.twitter.com/entries/77606-what-

is-retweet-rt (Last accessed on 3rd February, 2011)

21. 'RSVP', http://en.wikipedia.org/wiki/RSVP (Last accessed on 3rd February, 2011)
22. 'Introduction – What is SEO', http://www.webconfs.com/seo-tutorial/introduction-to-seo.php (Last accessed on 3rd February, 2011)
23. Bale, K., 'Top 10 Social Media Dashboard Tools', http://www.socialbrite.org/2010/11/09/top-10-social-media-dashboard-tools/ (Last accessed on 3rd February, 2011)
24. 'Facebook has a 420 Character Limit for Status Updates too', http://www.etiole.com/2010/03/facebook-has-a-420-character-limit-for-status-updates-too/(Last accessed on 4th February, 2011)

□

BIBLIOGRAPHY

1. Barefoot, Darren & Szabo, Julie. *Friends With Benefits: A Social Media Marketing* Handbook, 1st Edition: San Francisco: No Starch Press, Inc., 2010.
2. Evans, Dave. *Social Media Marketing: An Hour a Day*, 1st Edition, Indianapolis: Wiley Publishing Inc., 2008
3. Kotler, Philip; Armstrong, Gary; Agnihotri, Prafulla; & Haque, Ehsan ul. *Principles of Marketing: A South Asian Perspective*, 13th Edition, New Delhi: Dorling Kindersley (India) Pvt. Ltd., 2010.
4. Li, Charlene & Bernoff, Josh. *Groundswell: Winning in a World Transformed by Social Technologies*, 1st Edition, Massachusetts: Harvard Business Press, 2008.
5. Li, Charlene. *Open Leadership: How Social Technology can Transform the Way You Lead*, 1st Edition, San Francisco: Jossey-Bass, 2010.
6. Qualman, Erik. *Socialnomics: How Social Media Transforms the Way We Live and Do Business*,1st Edition, New Jersey: John Wiley & Sons, Inc., 2009.
7. Solis, Brian. *Engage: The Complete Guide for Brands and Businesses to Build, Cultivate, and Measure Success in the New Web*, 1st Edition, New Jersey: John Wiley & Sons, Inc., 2010.
8. Weinberg, Tamar. *The New Community Rules: Marketing on the Social Web*, 1st Edition, Sebastopol: O'Reilly Media Inc., 2009.

(Footnotes)

1. http://en.wikipedia.org/wiki/Avvaiyar
2. It is a travel brand formed by Merwyn Coutinho and Rajiv Rathod, wherein they travel the length and breadth of the county and share their stories, culture, places they visited with the community at large. They plan many road trips, camping and trekking. Source: http://www.furtherandbeyond.com

□□□